backstreet boys

CONFIDENTIAL

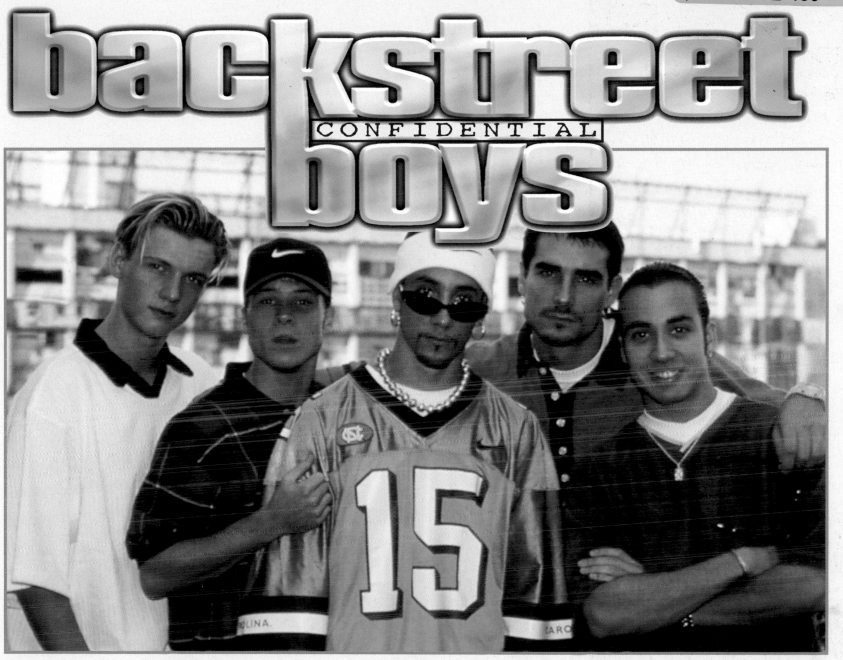

ANGIE NICHOLS

Billboard

First published in 1998 by Virgin Books

an imprint of Virgin Publishing Ltd

Thames Wharf Studios

Rainville Road

London W6 9HT

First published in the United States in 1998 by

Billboard Books, an imprint of BPI Communications Inc., at

1515 Broadway, New York, NY 10036.

Library of Congress Cataloging-in-Publication Data for this title can

be obtained from the Library of Congress.

ISBN 0-8230-7860-4

Printed and bound in Italy

Color origination by Colourwise Ltd

Designed by Stonecastle Graphics Limited

First printing 1998

1 2 3 4 5 6 7 8 9 / 06 05 04 03 02 01 00 99 98

Contents

Backstreet Boys Confidential

WITH ALBUM SALES OF MORE THAN TWENTY MILLION WORLDWIDE, BACKSTREET BOYS, BASED IN ORLANDO, FLORIDA, HAVE BECOME ONE OF THE MOST EXCITING MUSICAL SUCCESS STORIES OF THE LATE 1990S.

THEIR signature style includes heavenly five-part harmonies, a musical range that can smoothly shift gears from silky ballads to throbbing dance rhythms, and one of the most intricately choreographed stage shows to tour the world. But Backstreet Boys don't need to be flashy to impress. You only have to hear the members lift their voices *a cappella* – without musical accompaniment – to recognize the strength of their combined talents.

Tall, dark and handsome Kevin Richardson is the eldest and the most serious member. He's joined by his cousin Brian, who never lets his natural shyness get in the way of having fun. Nick, the group's youngest and a heartthrob to millions of young fans, is also the practical joker of the bunch. Flirty AJ is impossible to forget with his rapidly changing hairstyles and outrageous fashion sense. Finally, there's Howie D, or Sweet D as he's called, the group's sunniest personality and most charming conversationalist.

Whether you're a longtime fan or just getting acquainted with the fantastic five, now is your chance to learn all the confidential secrets of Backstreet Boys!

Chapter One

The Most Famous Group in the World

IT WAS 17 JULY 1998 AND THRONGS OF EAGER TEENAGERS WERE MILLING ABOUT IN FRONT OF NEW YORK'S HISTORIC RADIO CITY MUSIC HALL AWAITING ENTRY TO BACKSTREET BOYS' FIRST FULL-STAGE ARENA SHOW.

TICKETS had been impossible to obtain since way before the end of the school term in June. The show had sold out in an amazing 12 minutes.

After years on the verge of success at home, Backstreet Boys had finally conquered America. By the eve of their Radio City Music Hall gig, their self-titled debut album was certified four times platinum. Their third American single 'Everybody (Backstreet's Back)' had gone to number 6 in the Billboard top 100 singles chart and their video for the song was a firm favourite with viewers of MTV's *Total Request* show.

But as exhilarated as the fans were, the members of Backstreet Boys – Brian Littrell, Nick Carter, Kevin Richardson, Howie Dorough and AJ McLean – were twice as excited. Playing a show this big in New York was the realization of a long-harboured dream for Backstreet Boys. Although they had hosted larger concerts all over the world, New York City was a very big deal for them.

The group had played New York previously. After a concert in a smaller Manhattan venue, the Hammerstein Ballroom, in September of the previous year, Brian expressed surprise at his emotional reaction. 'Before the show I was thinking, "I'm not going to be nervous, it's just another show. I know it like the back of my hand,"' he said. 'And then, right before the curtain dropped, I was thinking, "This is New York City! This is America. Not only is this America, this is New York City! I mean, how rough and tough can you get? How American can you get?"'

It was just really strange. I clammed all up there for a second. Then I heard the music and I was like, it will be all right.'

Backstreet Boys aren't the first American group that needed to travel across the ocean to become famous, but they are the most recent. After following their dreams all across Europe, Canada and as far afield as Asia and Australia, the time was finally right to take it all back home.

By now the story of how five good-looking young men with gorgeous voices from Florida and Kentucky came together is a well-documented part of Backstreet Boys lore. Howie Dorough, AJ McLean and Nick Carter – all from Orlando, Florida – discovered their desire to entertain at very young ages. Howie had done some acting on TV shows and in films. AJ attended a performing arts school where he learned dance, music and acting. He had also gained some experience on the theatre stage and on television. Nick was primarily a singer who'd appeared in musicals and won several important competitions in his youth. By the time they were teenagers, all three were frequent faces on the Orlando audition and talent competition scene. AJ and Howie even had a vocal coach in common.

The early 1990s saw the demise of the chart-topping phenomenon New Kids On The Block, but one Florida businessman, Lou J. Pearlman, recognized the potential for creating a new group of good-looking guys who could sing and dance. Lou, cousin to 1970s singer Art Garfunkel of Simon and Garfunkel fame, had harboured musical dreams of his own but fate denied him the chance. He was determined to help some young performers achieve what he couldn't do for himself. Assembling a management team headed by Johnny and Donna Wright, former road managers for New Kids, he put out the call in search of rising stars.

'We had heard of a man named Lou Pearlman who was starting a label called Transcontinental Records and he was looking for talent,' remembers Howie. 'We were harmonizing, so we went in and auditioned for him. He suggested that we extend the group to five members.'

Enter Kevin Richardson. This native of Lexington, Kentucky had been living in the Orlando area searching for an entry into the music business. Born into a musical family, Kevin had sung in his local church and honed his skills as a

keyboard player and a vocalist in various cover bands for most of his teenage life. He'd come to Orlando with dreams of becoming a singer/songwriter in the manner of his musical idols Billy Joel and Elton John. To pay the rent while waiting for destiny to call him, he'd taken a job at Walt Disney World entertaining the

tourists by playing Aladdin in parades and dancing in a stage show dressed up as a Teenage Mutant Ninja Turtle.

A woman Kevin met on the Orlando club scene suggested he audition for a new R&B/pop vocal group she knew of. He auditioned and won a place in the newly christened Backstreet Boys – the name taken from the Backstreet Market, a now defunct outdoor flea market frequented by kids in the Orlando area.

'When one person takes the lead, the other person takes their harmony.'

As the band was still seeking a fifth member, Kevin made an excited phone call to his Kentucky cousin Brian Littrell, another veteran of Sunday choirs and school talent shows. After a frantic night of phone calls back and forth – and assurances by Donna Wright to Brian's parents that he would be tutored so that he could go on to receive his high school diploma – Brian arrived on the morning flight to Orlando the next day.

The chemistry among the five was immediate. 'We all got together and we worked on harmonies,' said Howie. 'It was cool because we're like five individual artists, five solo singers. When one person takes the lead, the other person takes their harmony.'

The Long Road To Fame

Critics who dismiss Backstreet Boys as an overnight sensation haven't done their homework. Lots of hard work and some major disappointments paved Backstreet Boys' road to fame.

The management team at Transcontinental Records decided that the best way to secure the group a deal with a major label was to get them widely seen and heard. So Backstreet Boys began by playing theme parks, parties, schools – any place that would let them perform. Gradually they built up enough of a following to be offered a high school tour across the country as ambassadors for Students Against Drunk Driving, or SADD.

If only videotapes were available of those early performances! 'When we were doing SADD in schools, we had a part of the show where we'd [play] Name That Tune,' recalled Kevin. 'We'd bring two or three girls up on stage and sit them down on stools and sing a Color Me Badd song, a Boyz II Men song and a Jodeci song and they'd have to guess. That was sort of entertaining, interacting with your audience,' he said. 'Being on the SADD tour before we even had a record deal really helped get our confidence up to get in front of people and sing.'

Along the way, Donna Wright was struggling to move heaven and earth in an effort to get record company

executives to come out and see Backstreet Boys. The group had released a single, 'Tell Me That I'm Dreaming', on their management's own independent Transcontinental label, but the song did not cause a stampede of offers. Donna was certain that the key to getting Backstreet Boys signed was their live performances. If the recording people could only see the reaction the Boys

aroused in the girls in the audience, they'd get a deal, she reckoned.

At one of their shows, she made a mobile phone call to the voice mail of a recording executive called Bobby Ducket, chiding him for not coming down to see the live show. Still on the phone, she signalled Howie to get the audience to scream. Not only did the girls oblige by rising to their feet and yelling loudly,

The Boys escaped from the adoring multitude by inches

they started scrambling out of their seats and running straight for Backstreet Boys! Shaken by the onrushing tidal wave of girls, but shrewd enough to not hang up the phone, Donna started shouting to their driver to bring the bus around. It was pandemonium! She and the Boys escaped from the adoring multitude by inches. And, it was all captured on the record executive's answering machine tape!

It's a little known fact that the first record label to sign Backstreet Boys was not actually Jive Records. Bobby Ducket and another executive David McPherson had paved the way for Backstreet Boys to be signed to Mercury Records. That's right, Mercury – the record label behind the teenage singing sensation Hanson. Ironically, Mercury reconsidered and dropped Backstreet Boys because they did not want to get involved with a young group! It was the first major disappointment for Backstreet Boys.

Still believing in the group, David McPherson took the act to Jive Records, who saw their potential and finally gave Backstreet Boys a home. 'I learned so much,' said Kevin of the experience. 'We were in a group and then we got management. They got us some shows and those shows got us some recognition. We were able to get in to see some record labels. They came out and saw our shows and that's how we got a record deal.'

'To be sitting in the car with my mom driving, and all of a sudden our song pops up on the radio – I'd been waiting and waiting for that day,' recalled AJ 'Boy, I just about cried.'

'We've Got It Goin' On' was released to radio simultaneously in the US and the UK in October 1995. The first time out (it was released a second time in Britain) it rose to a modest number 69 in the US singles charts and a slightly better 54 in the UK. Still, the group was very proud to hear themselves on the radio and see their single on sale.

'To me, to be sitting in the car with my mom driving, and all of a sudden our song pops up on the radio – I'd been waiting and waiting for that day,' recalled AJ 'Boy, I just about cried. It was like, whoa!'

For Nick, the ultimate thrill was seeing his photograph displayed in the CD racks of a record store for the very first time. 'The biggest surprise for me was to actually walk into a store and see your single sitting on a shelf,' he said. 'You can't believe it's you sitting next to all these other famous artists.'

But success in America didn't happen for Backstreet Boys straight away. The airwaves in the States were still saturated with the darker, angst-ridden sound of grunge and gangsta rap. Fun peppy dance songs were out. Romantic odes of unrequited love had few outlets. Backstreet Boys remained under-appreciated in a sonic landscape filled with the sounds of Nirvana, Pearl Jam and Snoop Doggy Dogg.

At the time, it was a big disappointment for the group from Orlando, but they're able to look back philosophically on it today. 'Back around '95 when we released "We've Got It Goin' On", it was basically gangsta rap and grunge. Our sound was, at least our first single, was like dance pop. It did pretty good on the club scene,' said Kevin. 'I think now, just like with fashion, it's run in a full circle in the music industry. We've got a lot of pop coming out right now. Just classic pop, almost like the '80s stuff coming back. So I think that helped us out.'

AJ added that their early disappointments taught Backstreet Boys an important lesson about the virtue of patience. 'You get what you want if you really work hard enough for it,' he said recently. 'If you have the patience to go through the hard days, the hard process, the hard work.'

Fortunately, in 1995 there were sunnier climates awaiting the Backstreet Boys across the Atlantic Ocean in the UK, Germany and the rest of Europe. 'It just blew up over there. America wasn't ready for a group like us,' said Howie. 'And over in Europe, they were just more accepting.

There were other groups around [with] the same kind of style. We came over with a very fresh, Americanized flavour. They just embraced us with open arms. I think it was just because we had a really fresh sound. We came across over there doing a lot of *a cappella* music in the very beginning, which was something kind of new for them.'

Backstreet Boys received the blessing of the influential UK music magazine *Smash Hits*. Its readers voted them Newcomers Of The Year in their annual poll in 1995. Soon, a bevy of other teen press accolades would follow.

As the group played gigs on their first tour, 'We've Got It Goin' On' was released for a second time in the UK in August 1996. This time it scaled the heights of

the record charts, peaking at number 3. A re-release of 'I'll Never Break Your Heart' (first released in the UK in December 1995) soon followed their first single's success, rising to number 8. Backstreet Boys had achieved two top 10 hits in only three months!

And the momentum was gathering pace in other parts of the world, too. Backstreet Boys mania grabbed teenagers in Germany, the first country where the Boys had trouble walking the streets without attracting masses of attention. German fans rewarded Backstreet Boys' frequent performances and extensive courting of the teen press with their very first platinum CD.

And it wasn't just Germany. Backstreet Boys were soon playing multiple performances in France, Spain, Amsterdam in The Netherlands, the Czech Republic, and all over Asia where the response to their soul-flavoured pop, hip-hop-styled dance moves and outgoing American personalities was overwhelming. Backstreet Boys may have seemed like just another 'boy band' at first glance, but they added their own innovations to break the mould. 'Every

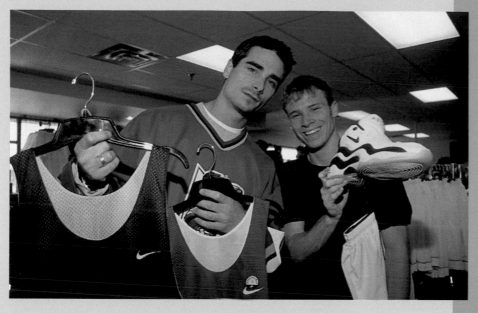

time we came around with a show we always took it to the next level,' said Howie. 'Our first major tour was with a band, unlike most groups over there that had just done it to a track. And our videos were always on the cutting edge. I think people looked at us as always being a step ahead of everybody.'

In 1996, the group also started to break in North America as their fame spread to the Canadian province of Quebec. 'It happened in Montreal in the French-speaking province first. One of the first big shows we did there was in front of 65,000 people [in St. Jean] at the Balloon Festival,' remembers Kevin. 'So, I mean, getting up in front of all those people – I'll never forget that. Canada holds a special place in our hearts.'

But their rise to fame hasn't all been a bed of roses. They've already weathered some potentially serious health problems

along the way. On tour in Germany, Kevin suffered an attack of appendicitis that needed immediate surgery and his enforced convalescence in a hospital far from home. Looking back, he admits that it was a miserable experience. And AJ's still trying to forget about the time in 1996 when he got too close to a moving van trying to escape a crush of Canadian fans, and instead had his toes crushed under its wheels. He spent the next month performing with his foot in a cast! Both Nick and Howie have fallen off stage, but fortunately escaped serious injury. And, Brian, well it's enough to say that Backstreet Boys' unrelenting schedule would take a serious toll on his health too, but we'll come back to that. By the end of 1996, the guys were all

noticeably thinner and a little more tired, but proud of all that they'd achieved.

As their fame spread all over the globe, Backstreet Boys and Jive Records still kept an eye on the evolution of popular music in America. They knew a time for Backstreet Boys' music would come there too. Although superstars abroad, the Boys never stopped courting the American press, even flying reporters over to see their performances and the reactions of their fans in other countries. It was a smart seed to plant in advance of the moment when Backstreet Boys would resume their long-delayed conquest of their homeland.

Chapter Two

Nick Carter
Confidential

BLOND-HAIRED, BLUE-EYED NICK CARTER CERTAINLY DOESN'T MIND THE ATTENTION HE RECEIVES FROM GIRLS. THE YOUNGEST MEMBER OF BACKSTREET BOYS HAS ALWAYS ENJOYED ATTENTION – WHETHER IT'S FROM THE GROUP'S YOUNGEST PRE-TEEN FANS OR THEIR MOTHERS WHO COME TO THE SHOW AND CHEER FOR THIS ADORABLE SINGER, OR ANY OF THE GIRLS IN BETWEEN.

nappies, thus beginning his fascination with video games).

Nick was joined four years later by sister Bobbie Jean, or BJ to her family and friends. He used to love to go to work with his dad, who spun records at the lounge at the weekends. The adorable blond toddler loved to get on the dance floor and boogie around for the customers. Nick was born with a passion for performing! His parents and the customers at the Yankee Rebel nicknamed the chubby baby 'Charlie Brown' after the *Peanuts* comic strip character.

Nick was born with a passion for performing!

NICK never felt the burden of his popularity more than any of the other guys, until a film phenomenon called *Titanic* debuted in December 1997. For the record, he finds the comparisons of his looks to those of *Titanic*'s star Leonardo DiCaprio just a little annoying. 'I get that all the time,' he said with a sigh in the summer of 1998. 'I take it as a compliment, but, you know, kind of not one that I like. I am my own person, so it is nice, but I am Nick Carter, not Leo.'

Nicholas Gene Carter was born on 28 January 1980 in Jamestown, a village in upstate New York whose previous claim to fame was as the birthplace of comedienne Lucille Ball, star of the 1950s television series *I Love Lucy*. When he was born, Nick's parents, Bob and Jane Carter, were helping his grandmother run a lounge called the Yankee Rebel. It was a smallish place with a little dance floor, a bar and a Pac Man video game (which Nick learned to play when he was still in

Nick boasts that his mother is the BEST cook in the world!

place in the *New Original Amateur Hour* in 1992.

At age twelve, Nick went to two auditions that would change his life. The first was for Backstreet Boys and the other was for the syndicated television variety series *The Mickey Mouse Club.* Filmed in Orlando, *The Mickey Mouse Club* has been a launching pad for child performers since the 1950s. Some of its recent successes include two members of the vocal group 'N Sync, Justin Timberlake and JC Chavez, as well as Jive Records solo artist Brittany Spears. When Nick received return calls from both the TV series *and* Backstreet Boys, who were not yet signed to a record label, he found himself with quite a decision on his hands.

Needless to say, Backstreet Boys won that fateful day. But Nick admits that he never realized how much work would be involved in joining a singing group like Backstreet Boys. 'A big lesson that we've learned is that it's not as easy as it looks, especially as we've been in the business for this long,' Nick has said. 'We first thought that you sign a contract, you get to go into the studio and you're handed a big check. It's not really like that. It's a lot of hard work. In the end, hopefully things will pay off. But, I mean, it's really not as easy as it seems.'

When Nick was almost six years old, his family packed up their old Cadillac Eldorado and moved south to the Tampa Bay area of Florida. Nick and sister BJ (now a model who in 1998 appeared in a video for the German musician Gil) were one another's best friends. Mischievous in the innocent way that only little kids can get away with, Nick recalls many mud fights, wrestling matches and duels (using wooden sticks for swords) during those years. Dad Bob worked at a senior citizen's retirement home which mum Jane cooked for – Nick boasts that his mother is the *best* cook in the world! Soon the Carter clan expanded with the birth of another sister, Leslie and finally the twins, Angel, a girl, and Aaron, his only brother.

In elementary school Nick won his first part in a school musical, *Phantom of the Opera*, completely by accident. Another student had been chosen for the role of Raoul but his singing voice wasn't strong enough to carry the part. Luckily, Nick was able to step in and take over. Although he was extremely nervous, he found that he really enjoyed being on stage.

That year, when he was nine, Nick started attending auditions for commercials and singing in local talent competitions. After appearing in ads for the Florida lottery and The Money Store, he decided that he'd rather be a singer than an actor. For two years, he was a featured vocalist during the Tampa Bay Buccaneers' (a local American football team) halftime show. He also won first

these guys.' Nick's unpredictability has even earned him the nickname 'Chaos' among the group.

Some of Nick's most fondly remembered practical jokes include the time he gave Backstreet's manager Donna Wright a stick of chewing gum which, unknown to her, turned her mouth and tongue a lovely shade of black. Another time, he stole all of AJ's clothes from his hotel room. At his own 16th birthday party, he called Howie over for a closer look at his birthday cake and pushed poor Sweet D's face into the whipped cream! Later in the evening, he and AJ (who was sharing in the birthday festivities as their anniversaries are so close together) got into a wrestling match that ended with them both plunging into manager Lou Pearlman's pool.

AKA Chaos

As the youngest member of the group, Nick has had to suffer his fair share of jibes from the other Backstreet Boys. But for every insult he's taken, he's played twice as many of his own jokes on the members of the group, their management team, their road crew, backing musicians and anyone else who has become part of his circle of friends. 'I'm definitely the prankster of the group,' he said in 1996. 'I like to do anything I can think of to

SUCH IS LIFE WITH BACKSTREET BOYS' MOST FAMOUS JOKER!

'I'm definitely the prankster of the group. I like to do anything I can think of to these guys.'

Nick will admit that the laughs he strives for are an attempt to hide his shy side. He and Brian are quite alike in this respect. Nick enjoys spending time alone. He'll rarely accompany the others on a night on the town, but prefers to stay in his hotel room watching a movie or playing video games.

Fans of Nick know that the part of his life that isn't reserved for Backstreet Boys or his family is preoccupied with video games. Although his favourite game changes frequently – his most recent obsession is *Mortal Kombat 4* – he's particularly partial to those involving adventure or sports. 'I like video games,' he's said in a classic understatement. 'I'm like, addicted to that stuff. I remember when I first played video games [the other guys] were always, "Get off that!" Now, it's cool. Sometimes I bring my Nintendo 64 or my Playstation [on the road]. It doesn't really matter.' In fact, in a 1998 interview Nick confessed that if the house he shares with his family were on fire and everyone was safe, the first

items he'd rescue would be his beloved game systems and a couple of game cartridges.

A lesser-known secret about Nick is that despite all the frequent air miles he logs in a typical year of travelling around the world with Backstreet Boys, he doesn't like flying. 'I just hate it, just plain hate it,' he's confessed. Even if the other guys opt to take a flight to the next city on their tour, Nick will often choose to stay with the bus and the trucks carrying their equipment and use the travelling time to play video games.

Nick also has a number of hobbies that don't involve television sets and joysticks. He loves to draw and will often doodle backstage before shows or during interviews with the

press. He never leaves home for a tour without his art supplies. For years, he's been happily engaged in a project to transform himself and the other members of Backstreet Boys into comic-book characters on his drawing pad. Don't be surprised if his tales of these Backstreet Boy superheroes see the light of day sometime!

'I like video games. I'm like, addicted to that stuff.'

When Nick is home in Tampa Bay, living in a house on the water that he shares with the rest of his family, he loves to absorb the serene beauty of the Florida coast. Whether it's cruising in the family boat, waterskiing or scuba diving (he's got his certification for deep-water dives), Nick's a true Floridian who enjoys the unspoilt wilderness of the Everglades.

At home, Nick drives a green Chevrolet truck and spends a lot of time with his siblings and friends. He still keeps in touch with Brent, his childhood best friend. He plays basketball and watches a lot of American football and baseball on television. His favourite teams are the Tampa Bay Buccaneers in American football and baseball's Oakland Athletics. For a night out, Nick loves movies and dancing to either hip-hop music or something really slow and romantic.

Naturally, Nick is very passionate about music. His tastes are extremely wide, too. 'My range is from old rock to alternative music to rap,' he's explained. 'I love R&B because that's what we sing. You should see my CD case. I have Wu Tang, Metallica, Journey. My favourite singer – he's almost my idol – is Steve

Nick has been eager to write some songs for the group's third album. However, his priority in the summer of 1998 was helping his only brother Aaron get started in his own music career.

Perry from Journey. I love Journey.' Another of his recent favourites is Puff Daddy.

But Nick's musical taste changes daily. 'It's just basically a mood. If I feel like listening to something one day, then I'm going to listen to it. If I wake up in the morning and I'm dressed like a gangsta, then I'm going to listen to rap that day,' he added. 'If I dress alternative, I'm going to listen to rock that day.'

An ear for music runs in Nick's family; in fact, his father Bob had his

own band when he was a teenager. Although he's never had formal lessons, over the past three years Nick has been teaching himself to play drums. He's even started incorporating a short drum solo into some of Backstreet Boys' live appearances.

Like the rest of the group, Nick has been eager to write some songs for the group's third album. However, his priority in the summer of 1998 was helping his only brother Aaron get started in his own music career.

Another Side of Nick

Questioned about the best and worst aspects of being in Backstreet Boys, Nick replied, 'All the people you get to see and the places you get to go. A lot of people out there don't get to do all the travelling that we get to do. We're very fortunate. That's one of the best things. The worst thing is probably just being away from home.' Home and family mean a lot more to Nick than most of his fans ever realize.

Backstreet Boys audiences in Germany were the first to be let in on the secret that Nick had an equally adorable younger brother who was also a singer. Aaron Carter, the family's youngest child, earned his own record deal at the age of ten and warmed up the audiences on Backstreet's American tour in the summer of 1998. The presence of his younger brother on tour brought out a more mature, paternal and caring side of Nick. 'I started at a young age, twelve, and I have gone through a lot, and he wants to do the same thing,' he said. 'Why not pass on everything that I know, and almost lead him past the rocky roads?'

Members of Backstreet's management team have marvelled at how Nick looks after his brother, and all his siblings, when they accompany him on tour. Be it Aaron or BJ, when Nick has family with him, he never leaves their side unless it's to perform.

And Aaron adores his older brother too. 'He gives me all kinds of advice,' he said. 'He gives me advice about how to perform on stage. Like, I pretend there's only two or three people in the audience.'

Managed in part by Nick, his mother Jane and several of Backstreet's managerial staff, Aaron scored three hit singles in Europe before releasing his self-titled debut in the United States in the summer of 1998. Of course, Nick is as proud as an older brother could be. 'Basically, he's a little blonde ten-year-old dancing fool,' Nick said fondly. 'I mean, I love him. He's my little brother and we have fun. It's pretty fun to see him up there performing.' Having realized so many of his own dreams with Backstreet Boys, Nick is anxious to help his little brother make all his wishes come true too.

Of course, Nick's not ready to pass on the torch to a new generation just yet. He still has a lot of dreams of his own to fulfil. Nick, and most of the other members of the group, would like to film a Backstreet Boys movie along the lines of Spice Girls' *Spice World*. Nick would also love to see his comic book published. He's writing songs both for Aaron to record and for the group. His greatest desire is to see one of his own tunes on Backstreet's third

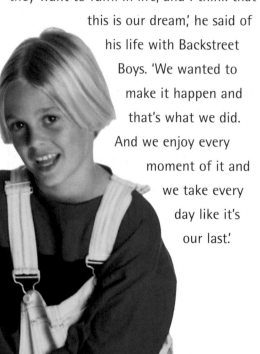

album. Most of all, Nick dreams of watching Backstreet Boys flourish as a respected vocal group well into the next century.

'I think everyone has a dream that they want to fulfil in life, and I think that this is our dream,' he said of his life with Backstreet Boys. 'We wanted to make it happen and that's what we did. And we enjoy every moment of it and we take every day like it's our last.'

NICK'S CONFIDENTIAL SECRETS

NICK LEARNED TO SCUBA DIVE AS A YOUNGSTER BECAUSE HIS DAD IS A CERTIFIED DIVE INSTRUCTOR. FATHER AND SON HAVE FREQUENTLY DIVED DOWN TO SHIPWRECKS OFF THE FLORIDA COAST.

In school, Nick always enjoyed History. If he could go back in time, he'd like to visit the medieval period.

HIS FAVOURITE COLOUR IS GREEN.

Believe it or not, Nick wasn't popular in junior high school. The other kids gave him a hard time because his singing made him miss so many days of school.

ONE OF HIS FAVOURITE ITEMS TO SHOP FOR IS DESIGNER TRAINERS.

Nick has a fear of insects and snakes.

If it were possible, Nick says he would enjoy sitting down for a chat with former US President Abraham Lincoln.

Nick is extremely ticklish!

It's possible to find Nick on the Internet – he often visits websites where computer games are available for downloading.

Nick thinks that actress Sigourney Weaver, who got tough as Ripley in the Alien movies, is a really cool lady.

Chapter Three

Our Dedicated Fans

EVERY PERFORMER WORTH THE PRICE OF A CD OR A CONCERT TICKET HAS ENOUGH COMMON SENSE TO ACKNOWLEDGE THEIR DEBT TO THEIR FANS, BUT BACKSTREET BOYS RECOGNIZE IT MORE THAN MOST. IT WASN'T SO LONG AGO THAT THEY WERE A STRUGGLING GROUP TRAVELLING ACROSS AMERICA IN A RUN-DOWN BUS TO PERFORM AT HIGH SCHOOLS.

BACK then, they had little say in the choice of the venues they played, the songs they sang or even the costumes they wore. The new respect they command and wealth they enjoy were all brought about by the loyalty of their fans across the world.

All five Boys were raised in modest circumstances, so their new affluence is still a pleasant surprise. Each has made generous gifts to his family: from Kevin paying off the mortgage on his mother's home, to Brian buying his brother a new car, to Nick's purchase of a boat for his parents and brother and sisters to enjoy. On the road, Backstreet Boys no longer have to contend with hours on the bus – they can fly to their next destination if they'd prefer. And being able to afford separate hotel rooms, everyone agrees, has made relations among the group members much easier. They never fought a lot, but having a little more privacy makes everyone much happier.

Success has given Backstreet Boys a lot more say about the direction of their careers, too. All five are writing songs they hope will be included in their third release. They're learning more about their work in the studio, too, having produced the song Brian wrote for *Backstreet's Back*. Their most recent videos are more representative of their personalities, particularly their creative video featuring monsters: 'Everybody (Backstreet's Back)'. Kevin dreamed up the concept on a plane flight. Expect to see more creative input from the guys themselves as Backstreet Boys recently renegotiated their contract with their management company to give them more control over all their future projects.

Backstreet Boys also have their fans to thank for getting the mainstream media to notice them. Their videos, once dismissed by MTV in the United States as too poppy and lightweight, are now finally getting regularly screened thanks to a flood of viewer requests. In Europe, they've won the MTV Select Award, which is voted for by viewers, two years in a row. And while their faces used to be seen smiling only on the covers of teen magazines, their rise to the top of the album charts in Europe and America has made larger circulation mainstream magazines finally take notice.

So when Backstreet Boys speak of their fans, it's always with huge love and gratitude. Their fans, however, are capable of some pretty crazy antics! And nobody knows this better than Backstreet Boys.

Dedicated Fans

Backstreet Boys call their most hardcore admirers their 'dedicated fans'. These are the girls who will fly halfway around the world just to see the members of Backstreet Boys for a moment at a recording session in New York City. Then, a week later, these same girls will appear in Germany at a radio appearance. The attention is flattering to the group, of course, but they also find it pretty funny that a bunch of 'normal' people like themselves should be the objects of such devotion.

The girls who cry uncontrollably when they get really close to a Backstreet Boy confuse AJ the most. He feels guilty for making them cry! 'I keep thinking, I'm just a regular guy. Why are you crying? Why weren't the girls crying all over me in high school? My God, I wish it had happened then,' he said with a laugh.

Even before they struck gold in America, European fans were finding ways of meeting Backstreet Boys – or their families – by travelling to the United States. Kevin explained that he has a large number of relatives in the Lexington area of Kentucky who all share the same last name. Most of them have had their phones changed to unlisted numbers because of frequent phone calls from fans.

Brian's mother has met several European fans who drove to Kentucky just to see where the Littrells lived. 'A little girl drove from Ohio [where she was visiting American relatives] to come visit my family in Lexington,' recalled Brian. 'They contacted my parents.' Brian's mother agreed to meet the girl and her family for breakfast that day. 'Because she went to all that trouble to bring a fan letter personally to my mother so I could get it, my mother would be like, "Brian Thomas! You write that girl back."'

Many of Backstreet Boys' parents have become local celebrities thanks to their famous sons. Brian's mother Jackie is a frequent on-air visitor at a Kentucky radio station keeping fans informed of what the group is doing. Meanwhile in Tampa, Nick's dad Bob gets a great vote of thanks from the owner of a local petrol station who's been doing a lot of business with tourists who stop in to ask for directions to Nick's house! For a while, another local man had his own Nick Carter enterprise selling maps to the family's house and even chartering a bus to take fans himself. 'They were getting 30 people a day at his poor little house,' related Brian. After fans picked all of the Carter family's flowers and even took some footballs and sporting equipment out of their yard for souvenirs, Nick's dad resorted to putting up a fence around their property.

'There were girls walking and jumping on soft top convertibles and putting holes in them!'

Nick's house really has become a landmark. It's appeared on the Internet and even at Backstreet Boys' concerts. 'We were performing, and some girl was holding this big poster,' recalled Kevin. 'It's a picture of Nick's house and it said "I was there!" It's amazing they can track us down like that,' he continued in disbelief. 'There was a fan letter to the whole group with pictures of girls sitting

on my car, Brian's car and standing in front of Nick's house. I found out on the Internet that there's a map to my mother's house in Kentucky!'

Despite all the hysteria around them, Backstreet Boys still like to meet their fans, pose for pictures and sign autographs – even sometimes at a risk to their own safety. AJ was pulled through a barricade once at the Royal Albert Hall in

London trying to make contact with his fans. 'He was standing up on the barricade, leaning over it, and it just tipped like that,' recalled Howie. 'He went out to kiss girls' hands or something like that.'

A near riot once broke out among fans waiting for their appearance on the German music television station, Viva. 'The mistake they made was that they publicized all week that Backstreet Boys were going to be there,' said Howie. 'The ruckus that caused! There was a lot of damage to cars. There were girls walking and jumping on soft top convertibles and putting holes in them!'

Added Nick: 'Our bus was white when we got there, and then [by the time we left] it was a giant wall of graffiti. They had markers. They wrote things like "I love you". After that incident, Viva asked Backstreet Boys *not* to come back soon!

In another incident early in their careers, Backstreet Boys were blamed for the uproar their presence caused in a record store. 'Things had taken off so fast that when we showed up they were expecting a couple of hundred people and there were 3,000 at a record store,' Brian remembered. 'It was a riot, let me tell you! We signed for five minutes – maybe six to ten autographs – and they busted through the barriers. It was like,

we *had* to leave. I was scared for my safety. Next thing I know, they're saying we cost this amount of money in damage because they didn't have enough security. They stole all the Backstreet Boys material that was in the store. We had cardboard cutouts, posters on the walls, they stole the CDs – it was a bad thing.'

Such a situation would never happen to the group today. Their managers are very strict about demanding adequate security. Backstreet Boys also employ their own bodyguards. They always travel with one for each of the group members.

The Boys have also learned from experience not to wear jewellery or clothing that can be pulled off easily at meet-and-greet opportunities with their fans. 'We've had hats pulled off. I was wearing a stocking cap once and it was pulled out to here,' said Brian indicating a spot several inches from his head. 'I finally thought, "if you want it so bad, you can have it."'

'Sometimes you try to get too close to give them what they want and you get something yanked off you.'

'It's not anything that's done intentionally,' AJ said. 'It's all accidental. They just want to touch you or get as close to you as they possibly can. And sometimes you try to get too close to give them what they want and you get something yanked off you or pulled or ripped out or whatever. But, you know, nobody's gotten really badly hurt, thank God. And hopefully nobody ever will.'

Another time Howie was waylaid by fans as he attempted to get through a crowd to the group's waiting tour bus. 'There were girls all behind this chain of [security] guys on either side,' remembers Nick. 'Howie came through and a girl grabbed him by the backpack. He was like a little turtle. I was right behind him. I stopped. Howie disappeared.'

Added Brian, 'They were pulling his hair. The neck of his shirt was all the way down to here.'

'It was nuts,' agreed Nick. 'They just want to touch you, but you don't realize what these little girls can do.'

After all these years, Backstreet Boys remain amazingly humble about the frenzy they create around the world. 'We're shocked. We're totally amazed when we pull up in front of hotels and venues and [the fans are] beating on the back of the bus and on the van and on the limousine,' said AJ 'It's a lot of fun and shocking and sometimes a little scary. But...our friends and our family, they keep our feet on the ground. And with each other, we try to keep each other in check so we don't get a big head or anything like that.'

Diversionary Tactics

So how are Backstreet Boys able to enjoy their social lives? Very cautiously! In Europe, they don't go anywhere without a security guard and that's starting to become the case in America as well.

They have resorted to climbing out of a least a few windows, sneaking through car parks and creeping down back staircases. Often, vans with blacked-out windows have been employed as decoys to lure fans away while the Boys make their escape by a different route. It's difficult and the group hates to do it, but sometimes it's the only way to ensure their safety and the safety of their fans.

When members of the group want a little privacy on a date or on a night out with friends or family from home, they stay clear of Hard Rock Cafes, Planet Hollywood restaurants or other places where the crowd is likely to be a younger one. Nightclubs, upmarket restaurants, and midnight movie theatres where the audience is less likely to be made up of teenagers are particular favourites of the group.

'We're always running around,' said Kevin. 'I like to check out the local music scene downtown [in Orlando]. I like to hear live bands. Lately I've been checking out this swing band. Me and AJ have going down and checking that out.'

For the members of the group who are old enough to do it (you have to be 21 to get entry to some clubs in the US), dancing at clubs still remains one of their favourite activities. 'It's hard after doing a show to just go to bed,' said Howie. 'You're all pumped up. Your adrenaline is going.'

One of the perks of stardom is not having to wait in lines at clubs; a benefit AJ, Howie and Kevin agree is a great advantage. They don't, however, like it when the patrons inside the club take special notice of them. 'People are really

'We enjoy having fun. So we go down, have fun, talk to anybody and dance.'

surprised at how we're so friendly,' said Howie. 'I guess a lot of people expect that when you get big you don't talk and you go to your room. We enjoy having fun. So we go down, have fun, talk to anybody and dance.'

These Boys love the limelight so much that they'll sing at a party at the drop of a hat. There's no false coyness with these guys! 'If there's a band or something, we'll get up there and sing,' said AJ 'I mean, just to have fun because it's a time where you're really not – in some ways you're being watched – but you're really not being watched, like by the press. This is just partying, a release, hanging out.'

Chapter Four

Brian Littrell
Confidential

BACKSTREET BOYS HAVE ALWAYS MAINTAINED THAT THEY ARE ONE GROUP WITH FIVE LEAD SINGERS. WHILE EACH MEMBER OF THE GROUP BRINGS HIS OWN SPECIAL TALENTS TO THE MIX, IT'S BRIAN'S HEAVENLY VOICE WHICH IS MOST PROMINENT ON BACKSTREET BOYS' GREATEST HITS, INCLUDING 'QUIT PLAYIN' GAMES (WITH MY HEART)' AND 'I'LL NEVER BREAK YOUR HEART'.

HE SANG HIS FIRST SOLO – BEFORE ALMOST 1,500 PEOPLE – WHEN HE WAS SIX OR SEVEN YEARS OLD.

IF NICK is the face of Backstreet Boys, AJ the showman, Howie the sweetness and Kevin the professionalism, then Brian is the soul of the group.

Brian Thomas Littrell was born on 20 February 1975 in Lexington, Kentucky into a family which loved music and was very active in its local church. Both his parents, Harold Jr, who worked for computer giant IBM, and his mother Jackie, who volunteered her time to their local parish, sang at Sunday services. 'I grew up in a big Baptist church, and ever since I could walk I was singing,' he remembered. 'I sound a lot like my dad. I hear my dad in me.'

Brian also has a brother, Harold III, who's three years older. Brian remembers that when his cousin Kevin Richardson used to visit, he'd watch the two older kids 'play rock stars'. Kevin, he recalled, would sing, while Harold would pound the drums.

Brian joined the children's chorus at his church Sunday school. He sang his first solo – before a congregation of almost 1,500 people – when he was just six or seven years old. Although he recalls being quite nervous, he also thoroughly enjoyed the attention. 'I'm very shy when it comes to meeting people,' he's said. 'But once I get to know a certain person, I can relax and then I turn into a ham.'

'I was very close to leaving home, pursuing college...I was hoping, maybe, to play basketball and be normal.'

But fate had another direction in mind for Brian.

Brian developed his talents in school musicals such as *Grease*. During his adolescence he was also fortunate enough to come under the influence of Barry Turner, a music teacher at his school who helped him hone his rich style. 'I had a black voice teacher [from] seventh grade all through eleventh grade who musically influenced me,' Brian recalled. 'He kind of got to mould me.'

Brian also continued to sing at his church where his voice and stage presence were widely praised, but initially that fame didn't impress his school friends. In the classroom, he was just another one of the guys.

That changed in his junior year of high school, when Brian's participation in a talent show made his classmates – and Brian himself – realize the extent of his natural talent. He and a female friend chose to perform a spiritual song called 'Another Time, Another Place'. Brian's gorgeous vocals caused so much screaming among the female members of the audience that he couldn't hear himself! That experience, he says, was a total rush and left him craving more.

Still, Brian's firmly middle-class upbringing found him looking forward to college as he reached the last of his high-school years. When the fateful call from his cousin Kevin that brought him into Backstreet Boys arrived – pulling Brian out from his US History class – he was completely unprepared. 'I had no expectations because I really had no idea what I was getting myself into,' he recalls. 'I was 18 years old. I was very close to graduating high school. I was offered a singing scholarship to the University of Cincinnati Bible College.' Brian had his future already planned. 'I was going to go to Cincinnati, which is only 100 miles from Lexington, so I would be close to home, yet away from home,' he recalled.

NOW, HE SPENDS MUCH MORE TIME SETTING HIS THOUGHTS TO MUSIC WITH HIS GUITAR.

Backstreet Boys to see one of his own tunes appear on one of their albums. 'That's What She Said' was released on their second European CD, *Backstreet's Back*. Although the song wasn't included on their debut CD in the United States, Brian introduced it to American fans as the highlight of his solo spot on their summer 1998 concert tour.

While all five Backstreet Boys have taken a greater interest in songwriting as they approach their third CD, Brian has changed his work habits the most radically to find time to write. He's never been into clubbing or the sort of guy who likes late-night parties, but he used to spend a lot of time chatting on the phone, watching movies in his hotel room or playing video games with Nick far into the night. Now, he spends much more time setting his thoughts to music with his guitar or with the help of some of the musicians from Backstreet Boys' backing band.

AKA B-Rok

Although he was the last member to join Backstreet Boys, Brian's participation in the group has helped shape their popular R&B/pop sound. Influenced by favourite performers such as Luther Vandross, Boyz II Men, Take 6, and The Temptations, Brian's blue-eyed soul has been the foundation for some of their most popular songs.

Brian is also taking shape as a songwriter. He was the first member of

Brian's blue-eyed soul has been the foundation for some of their most popular songs.

'Athletics have always been an important part of my life... It relieves the stress.'

But no matter how hard he works on his music, Brian still makes time for fun. His fans know that this star athlete is never far away from a basketball. It's a sport that all of the members of Backstreet Boys enjoy, but one that Brian especially excels at. 'Athletics have always been an important part of my life,' he said. 'I like making out [basketball] plays and I bring a basketball on the road. So any time we have, if we see a park or if the weather's nice, we can get out and play. It relieves the stress.'

The other Backstreet Boys christened Brian 'B-Rok'. 'Because he likes to play basketball, and they call basketballs rocks,' explained his best buddy Nick.

Among the Backstreet Boys, Brian and Nick are inseparable, prompting one of their security detail to nickname them 'Frick and Frack' (Brian is Frick, Nick is Frack). The pair enjoy sports, girls, music and movies. They also share a mischievous love of pranks and a similar sense of humour. They even have their own secret handshake. Although both are

reputed to have somewhat short tempers, flare-ups between them never last more than a moment. In fact, more than one of their disputes was settled on the basketball court!

Brian calls Nick and the other members of the group his brothers, but he hasn't forgotten the folks he left behind in Kentucky. He calls home often and has flown his parents all over the world – most recently to Spain in 1998 – to see his shows. His brother Harold has crossed thousands of miles of Europe with

Backstreet Boys. 'I brought my brother out on tour once,' recalled Brian with a grin. 'He wanted to meet all the girls!'

No matter how many miles are between him and home, Brian always keeps with him the morals and good sense his family taught him. 'I'm not real religious but my family brought me up with a religious background,' he said. 'I try to stay focused on that and do my own thing.' One of Brian's favourite ways of winding down after a long day of interviews, photo sessions and meeting the crowds is by reading a bit from a book that has travelled with him around the globe. 'There's a book of proverbs from the Bible – it's a book that my parents gave me a while ago,' he revealed. 'They're just quotes and sayings of the day to keep your feet on the ground and keep your thoughts together. It's nice to go back to your hotel room after a long crazy day and read a page or two.'

Heartache

Brian's devotion to his family and his faith was strengthened by a childhood illness that nearly ended in tragedy. Born with an undiagnosed murmur and a hole in his heart, Brian was always a happy athletic kid who never had any trouble keeping up with the other children in the neighbourhood. At five, he took a tumble from his Big Wheel tricycle that his doctors later assumed signified the start

of a bacterial infection that began circulating in his blood. Nevertheless, Brian seemed perfectly fit. A few weeks later at his grandparents' house, Brian was messing around with his older brother when he slipped and fell, sustaining a nasty bump to his head. Worried that he might have concussion, his mother took him to the hospital where the doctors discovered Brian's affliction.

Brian was admitted immediately and started on a course of medication that doctors doubted would cure him. The

infection had gone too far, they said. The doctors actually told Brian's parents to prepare themselves for the worst. But faith sustained his family as Brian remained in hospital for two months gradually recovering. Not only was it the loneliest time of his life, but he admits that he sometimes still has nightmares about it. The doctors called Brian's recovery nothing short of a miracle. 'I think everyone is here for a reason,' Brian has said. 'I think it's destiny why we're all here together.'

Since his childhood ordeal, Brian has submitted to yearly cardiac examinations to monitor his health. He has always understood that some day he might have to undergo the surgical procedure to close the small hole in his heart. Over the past years as a member of Backstreet Boys, Brian kept up with the others as they danced and sang for fans all over the world. But by early 1998, he'd begun to feel tired. When his doctors at his annual checkup recommended that he take time off for the operation, Brian finally agreed.

'It was just like a wake-up call to make you appreciate every day what you have and not take things for granted.'

'It was just like a wake-up call to make you appreciate every day what you have and not take things for granted,' said cousin Kevin just weeks after Brian's operation. The surgery, which took place on 8 May 1998, was extremely successful. Brian's doctors recommended that he be given six to eight weeks off to recuperate, begin physical therapy and allow the hospital to do tests to determine the success of the procedure.

On 8 July, Brian appeared on stage with Backstreet Boys in Charlotte, North Carolina for the start of their very first arena-scale tour in America. It was exactly the moment he'd been dreaming about all summer. 'I can be on stage in front of thousands of people and there's a point in the show – it doesn't matter how loud the audience is, but you can hear a pin drop on stage because you're in such a world,' he's said. 'You're focused. You don't think about the lyrics or what's going on on stage. You just glance out into the audience and the lights go out and the lighters or those little glow sticks

come on. It's just such a sense of fulfilment inside.'

Despite his success with Backstreet Boys and even the physical odds he's overcome to get to the stage, Brian remains very modest, even humble. 'I question myself every show. "Why are these people here?" I never dreamed of being a big star or anything, but to be a singer, to do sometime I love, to go to work every day and do something I enjoy, that's what I was looking for,' he said. 'It's what you make of it. I mean, I'm no different than anyone else. Everyone has different qualities and everyone is here for a reason.'

The thrill of winning awards, receiving platinum albums or counting up the number of times he's seen his face on the cover of magazines pales in comparison with the joy Brian gets from entertaining people. 'We want to be perceived as five guys who love to sing, love to perform and love to share the gifts of music that we have with the whole world,' he said.

BRIAN'S CONFIDENTIAL SECRETS

It will never replace basketball, but Brian's new favourite sport is golf.

Brian wears a tattoo of a cross on his left shoulder. He says getting it done didn't hurt much.

Brian refuses to go on rollercoasters because he is afraid of heights.

Brian carries a stuffed toy dog for company on the road.

BRIAN ENJOYS READING MYSTERY NOVELS.

Brian and Nick wrote a song for Aaron Carter's debut CD called 'Ain't That Cute'.

If he hadn't become a singer, Brian would have loved to play professional basketball.

He most dislikes people who are phony and liars.

BRIAN BITES HIS NAILS! HE SAYS IT'S PRETTY EMBARRASSING WHEN HE'S SIGNING AUTOGRAPHS AND FANS COMMENT ON IT.

Chapter Five

Backstreet Boys Bring it Home

AT THE BEGINNING OF 1997, NICK, AJ, HOWIE, BRIAN AND KEVIN COULDN'T WALK DOWN A STREET IN MUNICH WITHOUT BEING SURROUNDED BY FANS. WHILE SHOPPING IN LONDON THEY EMPLOYED DIVERSIONARY TACTICS TYPICAL OF A SPY NOVEL TO EVADE THE PRESS.

AND in Montreal, the Boys had to escape by way of a tunnel underneath Molson Arena to avoid the jam of excited fans their concerts would inevitably cause in the city streets.

Yet Backstreet Boys could still visit a shopping mall in Orlando virtually unrecognized. In New York, the only time they'd be asked for autographs was when they passed by the tourist attractions that drew foreign visitors. A B-movie actor in Los Angeles still attracted more attention from celebrity hunters than any of the Backstreet Boys in the early months of 1997, although they were superstars in other parts of the world.

Of course Backstreet Boys were not ungrateful for the success they'd achieved in so many places – they love their fans no matter where they live – but it was impossible not to want to achieve a similar triumph in the place they called home. So many of the guys' extended families had never seen the full impact of a live Backstreet Boys performance before a thunderous audience. Howie, the group's unofficial cameraman, continued to videotape their triumphs around the world, but watching on TV didn't have the same impact. There were also so many other people the guys wanted to make proud of them – from the choir directors of their youth, to neighbours who babysat for them, to the kids they played baseball with in fourth grade at school.

'It's a chance for us to show all of our friends and family what we've been doing for the past four or five years since we've been together,' said Kevin about succeeding in America. 'It's a personal thing for us.'

'I just think it's a long-awaited homecoming. I'm really excited to see it happen this year,' said Howie in early 1997. 'I think we're definitely ready for it. We've had a chance to really hone our craft and to appreciate all our fans and all the magazines and press who stuck behind us and kept the word going back home.'

The early part of the New Year was spent recording their second European album *Backstreet's Back* in the United States, Britain and Sweden. That spring, the group promoted their follow-up album with a round of concerts and television appearances in Europe and Canada. They also flew back to the US for television appearances on shows such as *Saturday Night Live*, and a chance to ride a float in New York's annual Macy's

Thanksgiving Day Parade which is televised all over the country.

Backstreet Boys launched their bid for fame in America in earnest in the summer of 1997, by releasing the single 'Quit Playin' Games (With My Heart)' and celebrating with a worldwide television audience in a broadcast from Times Square in New York City. The single would rise to number 2 in the singles charts, coinciding nicely with the long-awaited release of their debut CD *Backstreet Boys* in America on 12 August 1997.

Containing the most popular songs from

Backstreet Boys' two European releases, the album presented a unique journey of sound illustrating the evolution of the group. 'It's like the best of what we've been doing for the past two years,' said Kevin at the time. 'The album has five of our singles that we released in Europe already – which were great songs – and we have some really great new songs added.'

AJ pointed to the variety of songs on *Backstreet Boys* as the reason for its potential to appeal to so many different kinds of people.

'We cover every group of every age of every race ... going from one song that is a dance song to one that is a ballad to one that is a mid-tempo R&B type song. We don't just specifically cover one type.'

The summer of 1997 would have undoubtedly belonged to Backstreet Boys if the juggernaut of a band of three brothers from 'the middle of nowhere' had not burst on the scene. Hanson's irresistibly catchy tune 'MMMbop', a song reminiscent of the early Jackson Five, erupted on the airwaves to catch the ears

of young and old alike. Backed by unprecedented media attention for a group so young and a promotional tour of malls across America, Hanson caught fire in 1997. The brothers ended the year on a high note with a good-natured appearance in a skit on *Saturday Night Live* where they allowed themselves to be held at gunpoint in an elevator by two characters who claimed to have been driven mad by the constant repetition of 'MMMBop' on the radio that summer. The entire nation could relate to that!

But Hanson weren't the only ones grabbing headlines. With their own irresistible song, cute nicknames, in-your-face attitude, and a rallying cry of 'Girl Power', the Spice Girls landed on American shores in the summer of 1997. Who could resist them? Within the three-minute span of the adorable video for 'Wannabe', Americans forgot 200 years of

history and immediately surrendered to the British – the British queens of pop, that is. It was just that kind of a summer.

Backstreet Boys received a lot less press but they were still thrilled to celebrate the success of 'Quit Playin' Games'. They were content to bide their time. 'I really believe that [because] the five of us want it bad enough, we'll be where Hanson is right now eventually,' said AJ that June.

Backstreet Boys' more gradual advance into the American public's consciousness may have been a blessing. Let other groups chase each other to become the flavour of the month, the group reasoned, Backstreet Boys were looking to be around for more than just one summer.

'I think we just want people to respect us for our music first and then look at us however they want to look at us. We're not perfect. We're just a bunch of regular Joes that just want to do

something that they love,' said AJ. 'If people look at us as just being normal, which is what we are, then that's cool. If they look at us as being teen idols, then that's cool. We're all about being positive but it's all about the music'.

Backstreet Boys were working hard on two fronts – domestically in the US and also by promoting their second CD in Europe. They continued their tradition of innovative videos that June when they arrived in California to film one for 'As Long As You Love Me'. They had come to Pasadena, less than an hour's drive from downtown Los Angeles, to employ the state-of-the-art technique of 'morphing' which the wizards of Hollywood had created for the movies. The finished video, where viewers could watch Howie morphing into Nick who becomes AJ, who becomes Kevin, who changes into Brian, is a truly original and extremely enjoyable addition to Backstreet Boys' already impressive video library.

One week later, the Boys found themselves in yet another warehouse-sized studio filming the video for 'Everybody (Backstreet's Back)' specifically for the European market. That video, which turned the fantastic five into ghoulish but lovable monsters, was the first concept to originate from within the group. As the Boys recall, the germ of the idea started with Kevin on a plane ride when he imagined that it would be fun to do a sort of 1990s version of Michael Jackson's 'Thriller'. The other members of the group jumped in suggesting which monsters everyone should be. Although Kevin decided to play Dr Jekyll and Mr Hyde, Nick thought he would have made a great Frankenstein.

The year ended with more concert appearances, both in Europe where the Boys headlined, and in America, where they joined other groups such as Chumbawumba, Savage Garden and Hanson for short-set, multi-act holiday benefit concerts. AJ admitted that having to work hard to get Backstreet Boys' name out in the States felt really good.

'I'd like to go back to my roots and struggle to become something instead of having it almost handed to us on a silver platter,' said AJ. 'Now, it's a challenge to break here in the US. We have a reason to work harder – a reason to have the fire in our eyes again. And all of us do. We want it bad here now. We know we've got it in Europe, can we have it on homebase?

Clearly, AJ had given some thought as to why the States is such a hard market to break. 'They are so fickle!' he said of American listeners. 'You read a *Billboard* here and it's like country, R&B, pop, this, that. It's like everything is categorized'.

The Christmas season of 1997 was the first time since the early days that Backstreet Boys were able to go home for a month's stay. The group were all looking forward to being able to shop for gifts for their families at a more leisurely pace – rather than having to do it all on Christmas Eve! 'This Christmas is going to

'I'd like to go back to my roots and struggle to become something instead of having it almost handed to us on a silver platter.'

IT'S GREAT TO BE BACK HOME, CALL YOUR MUM UP AND SAY, "WATCH THE SHOW TONIGHT, I'LL BE ON"

popped up for a cameo appearance on the ABC family comedy series *Sabrina, The Teenage Witch.*

'It's great to be back home, call your mum up and say, "Watch the show tonight, I'll be on,"' said Brian.

'We've done television shows all over the world but ... it's like you don't realize,' said Kevin. 'You might do a show that's got a viewing audience ten times the size of *Regis & Kathie Lee* but you really wouldn't know because you don't live there. When you live here, you realize it and call home and your family sees it and your friends see it. It means a lot.'

Radio picked up the ball that Backstreet Boys had lobbed and ran with 'As Long As You Love Me'. It peaked at number 4 on the Hot 100 Airplay charts in March. On the strength of the single, their CD moved up to number 8 with a bullet on *Billboard*'s Top 200 album chart. Things were getting pretty exciting!

be good!' Kevin said delightedly in October. But Backstreet Boys' business couldn't wait until the new year. On 26 December, the guys flew to Canada for a set of shows that would take them to Halifax, Nova Scotia, Toronto and Montreal.

As 1998 dawned, Backstreet Boys continued to spread the message of their music through appearances on American television. Highlights included their performances on *Live With Regis and Kathie Lee* (where they made the national TV debut of 'As Long As You Love Me'), *ABC In Concert*, *The Ricki Lake Show*, *The Rosie O'Donnell Show* and Nickelodeon's variety show for kids, *All That*. They even

'The fact that things are going so quickly is what's blowing my mind.'

'I couldn't be happier,' said AJ that spring. 'Hopefully things keep going like a locomotive and it just doesn't ever stop. Every time we leave and come back to the US something always seems to be bigger and better.'

'Everybody (Backstreet's Back)' was released as a single in April. It too, was well received by radio stations. The catchy song rode high up the charts coming to a rest at number 4, while the group's accompanying monster mash video – finally released in the US – was a frequent selection on MTV's viewer call-in show.

'Shocked! Shocked! I'm more or less shocked at how quick things are moving,' said AJ at the time. 'The fact that things are going so quickly is what's blowing my mind.'

But promoting their album wasn't the only thing on Backstreet's minds. That winter, Orlando had been hit by ferocious tornadoes that left many homeless. Despite a hectic itinerary that had Backstreet Boys scheduled to fly from Jamaica, where they played at MTV's spring break festivities, to Ireland to start their European tour, the group unanimously agreed to make a detour home to join Orlando Bands Together, a benefit concert. Backstreet, along with fellow Florida acts 'N Sync, L.F.O., No Mercy and Vanilla Ice among others,

raised $250,000 for the tornado victims, before being escorted by an Orlando police motorcade back to the airport to catch their flight to Dublin.

By early summer, Backstreet Boys were back in the US drawing out the big guns with the release of their fourth single, 'I'll Never Break Your Heart', an accompanying video filmed in West Hollywood, and the debut of their first long-format home video in the United States. *Backstreet Boys All Access* is comprised of behind-the-scenes footage of the making of their 'As Long As You

Love Me' and 'Everybody (Backstreet's Back)' videos as well as interviews with the group, choice video clips from their entire career and two live performances from Europe. In all, a pretty perfect present to their fans.

Continuing their effort to reach out to every man, woman and child with their glorious five-part harmonies, Backstreet Boys scheduled appearances on extremely diverse programmes. The Backstreet summer battleplan included stops at the time-honoured late-night talk programme *The Tonight Show With Jay Leno*, *The Magic Hour*, a new entry into late-night TV hosted by former pro basketball sensation Magic Johnson, and daytime TV's *The View*, whose audience is dominated by retired people and stay-at-home women. Clearly, no one in America was being allowed to live the summer without a glimpse of Backstreet Boys!

In July, the final phase of the Backstreet Boys invasion began as the group played the first shows on their ambitious 33-date American arena tour which would take them from Seattle, Washington to Grand Essex, Vermont and all points in between. 'Slowly but surely we're building a nice big fan base', said Kevin a few weeks before the start of the tour. The goal, he said, is to 'build it slowly and create a good foundation and build something that's going to be here for a long time. So we're excited.'

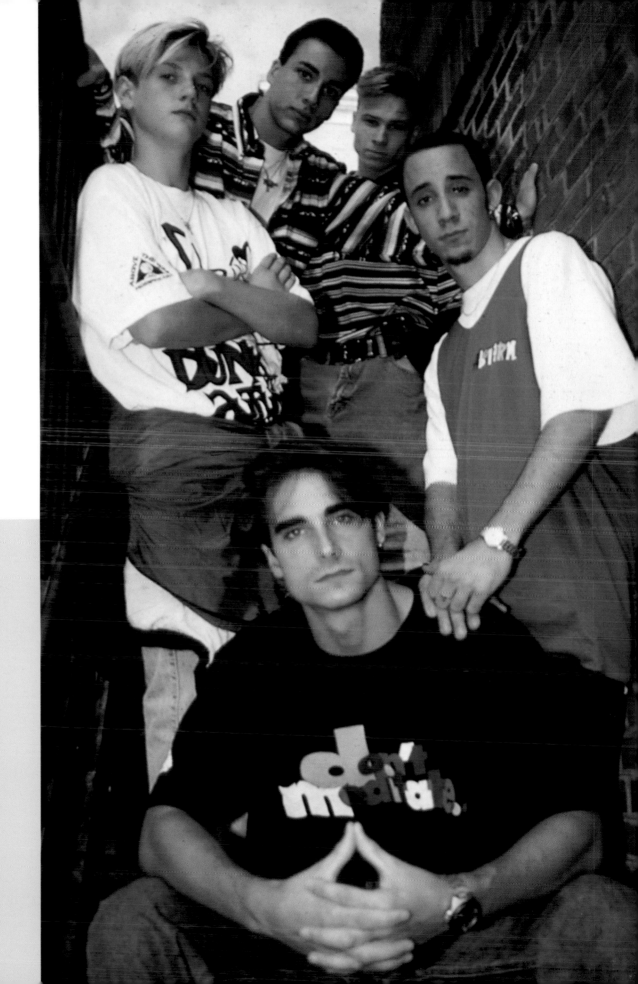

Chapter Six

Howie Dorough
Confidential

NONE OF THE MEMBERS OF BACKSTREET BOYS DESERVES HIS NICKNAME MORE THAN HOWIE, AKA SWEET D. HE'S A TOTAL DARLING WHO MAKES FRIENDS EASILY AND WILL TALK TO ABSOLUTELY ANYONE!

THERE'S not a shy bone in this performer's body. What's more, Howie is rarely in a grumpy mood, is supremely confident yet modest, and is always happy to be doing his part to make sure Backstreet Boys remain one of the world's most popular vocal groups.

Certainly the credit for Howie's well-balanced personality belongs to his large, supportive family. Growing up as the youngest of five siblings, he received a lot of love, attention and the encouragement to go after his dreams. Howard Dwaine Dorough was born on 22 August 1973 in Orlando, Florida to Hoke, a police officer, and Paula, a housewife. He admits that his older sisters and brother – Angela, Caroline, Polly Anna and Johnny – doted upon him. With ten

years between himself and his brother, Howie was definitely treated like someone special.

But sweet-natured Howie would never have grown up into the great guy he is today without a bit of discipline. That's where his father, who retired from the force when Howie was twelve, came in. His dad, Howie has said, was strict in the sense that he always expected his children to be accountable for their actions. He's a really great dad, Howie has said.

Family means the world to Howie. He's flown his parents out to see Backstreet Boys shows all over the world. His sister Polly Anna frequently accompanies him on the road, but when she doesn't, he calls home a lot. Howie

never leaves home without his phone card. 'I'm pretty close to my family – we're one of those tight families,' he's said with pride.

In every country he's visited, Howie takes time out to buy gifts for the people back home. 'I'm Mr Souvenir man! My mom collects elephants, so normally wherever I go I get her an elephant. One of my older sisters wants postcards, so I send her a postcard from whatever country we visit. My little nieces like those little dolls dressed up,' he said. 'By the time I go home I have to get an extra suitcase to carry everything. But it's cool.'

Most Likely to Succeed

Evidence of Howie's singing talents appeared when he was just learning to walk. At the age of three, he used to jump up on his grandmother's bed with a little guitar and sing his favourite song, 'Baby Face'. Howie, however, thought he'd become a police officer like his dad, or a doctor, like his uncle, until his older sister Polly Anna unintentionally intervened.

'My sister's been an inspiration to me,' Howie has said on numerous occasions. 'She's an actress and a singer also, so she got me started in the business.'

When Howie was in first grade he went to his first audition with Polly Anna, who was a senior in high school and aspiring to a career in entertainment. To everyone's surprise, they both won roles in a community theatre production of *The Wizard of Oz*. 'I was a Munchkin,' he recalled. 'She was Glenda the Good Witch.'

As he grew a little older, Howie sought out the company of other kids in his school who were passionate about the arts. He auditioned for roles in his school's plays, took lessons with a singing instructor and joined an acting troupe for kids called Show Stoppers. During this time he discovered his amazing falsetto voice which today punctuates Backstreet Boys' songs. Even after his voice changed, he was able to hit higher notes than most of the girls in his vocal class. Howie also earned valuable experience singing in the children's choir of the Roman Catholic Church that his family attended, and later, the men's choir and the chorus at school.

But singing wasn't Howie's only early ambition. He wanted to try his hand at acting too. He attended many auditions in the Orlando area and even won some roles. Look closely for a scene that takes place in a classroom near the end of the 1989 movie *Parenthood* to see a fourteen-year-old Howie in a non-speaking role. He also had a small part in the film *Cop and a Half*. His other acting credits include several commercials for Disney World as well as a role in a TV pilot called *Welcome Freshman* for the children's cable TV channel Nickelodeon.

Howie admitted that he could easily have traded his microphone and dancing shoes for a chance to become an actor. 'Acting and singing are like one for me. I was either going out for an acting audition or I was in a talent competition,' he remembered. 'I tried to keep them both equal so whichever one took off first was the one I was going to go with.'

In making the rounds of auditions and talent shows, Howie became friends with future Backstreet Boy AJ McLean. 'We met up with each other in Orlando through a talent competition,' he explained. 'We had a vocal coach that I used to work with who was, at the time, his vocal coach. He introduced the two of us.'

It wasn't long before Howie and AJ noticed another young performer on the audition circuit, a little blond bundle of energy named Nick Carter. 'We kept running into each other all the time there at auditions,' Howie recalled. 'We all did stuff for Nickelodeon, Disney, MGM Studios. We met through acting and found out we had a passion for singing. So we put a little group together and then took it to a small record label in Orlando.' Of course, the seed that trio planted would grow into Backstreet Boys.

'My sister's been an inspiration to me, she's an actress and a singer also, so she got me started in the business.'

'Howie's been the group's chief ambassador to a world of new fans.'

AKA Sweet D

Although he's no longer acting, Howie plays many roles within Backstreet Boys. He's the peacemaker who will help smooth out the occasional squabbles that occur among the guys. He's also the group's social director because he loves the nightlife! Finally, as Backstreet Boys prepare to take their music into new countries such as Mexico and Brazil, Howie's been the group's chief ambassador to a world of new fans.

It's not a surprise. The other band members praise Howie's gift for diplomacy. 'Howie's Mr. Mediator,' said AJ 'Just like, "C'mon guys, let's be serious,

DANCING HAS

ALWAYS BEEN A

PASSION FOR HOWIE

let's be focused."' Somehow, Howie's even temper and rational manner make him able to say such things without hurting anyone's feelings.

Of all the guys, Howie's the least likely to get angry or to let stress affect his sunny personality. There is, however, one way to break his calm surface. According to AJ, Howie hates to have his hair touched! Messing with his curly

locks – especially when he's just leaving for a night on the town – is definitely looking for trouble!

Dancing has always been a passion for Howie and he likes nothing better than to go out clubbing after a long day of photo sessions and interviews. He particularly loves salsa and hip-hop dancing. Early in the history of Backstreet Boys, Kevin was his frequent companion, but more recently it's AJ who's been his partner-in-crime.

Of course, if Howie's sister Polly Anna is travelling with him, she's sure to be along for a good time too. 'When you're in town you want to hang out. It's always good to have company. It's nice to have somewhat of a normal social life', he said. 'It's kind of cool because you meet certain people in different countries who always show up to shows and take you out to clubs and show you around the city and stuff'.

Howie jumps at the opportunity to experience different cultures. When the start of Backstreet Boys 1998 European tour found the group in Dublin, Ireland on St. Patrick's Day, Howie knew he couldn't stay shut in his hotel room. After all, through his father he's fully one-half Irish himself! He and a couple of the Backstreet Boys' entourage sneaked out in a van to join in with the fun. It was a great time. Howie and his friends were able to enjoy most of the parade's floats before too many people recognized him. Although he graciously posed for some photos and signed autographs, it wasn't long before his security advisor suggested it was time to leave.

Ever-curious Howie loves the experience of world travel that his membership of Backstreet Boys has allowed him. 'Normally, the first time we're in countries, when we're doing press, that's when we get to see the culture', he explained. 'Sometimes we try to coordinate with the press to do photo sessions at landmarks. That way we can see some of the sights. The best thing [about being in Backstreet Boys] is getting a chance to travel around the world to see new places, see new cultures and try new foods.'

While Brian, Nick and especially AJ seek out typical American fare – hamburgers from McDonald's preferably – wherever in the world they are, Howie and Kevin are more adventurous. Be it sushi in Tokyo, satay in Bangkok or bangers and mash in London, Howie's always excited to try something new.

For the past few years, Howie has been urging Backstreet Boys to take their music to new parts of the world, particularly Latin markets such as South America. Now it's happening. 'I'll Never Break Your Heart' was the first Backstreet Boys video to be filmed in both English and Spanish versions. 'I've tried to influence the guys into translating a couple of our songs into Spanish,' Howie said. 'I think that it's a really big market out there and I'm thinking that so many American groups like us can really cash in on that. A lot of people listen to music when it's from the heart.'

Moving into the Latin markets isn't just good business sense from Howie's perspective, it's also a way of respecting his heritage. 'I think it's personal [since] I'm part Spanish because my mom's Puerto Rican. It's part of my blood that I want to reach out to everybody out there,' he says.

In May 1998 when Backstreet Boys took the first extended break of their career, Howie flew to Mexico and Brazil to promote Backstreet Boys. It was his first solo trip on behalf of the group and quite a strange experience. Although he took his sister Polly Anna along for company, he confessed that it felt very odd not to have Nick, Brian, AJ and Kevin with him for the journey. 'When I did the trip to South America without the rest of the group, that was when it really hit me, the loneliness of not having the four guys around me,' he said. 'You appreciate the things you take for granted, like having a big group to be with. It is good to have the five of us bonding with each other. We usually don't have our families with us, so that is why it is good to have brothers like these guys and to be so close.

'We look out for each other and we always have each other to be with.'

The Future

While his promotional trip without the group made Howie realize that he's not ready for a solo career right now, he is not afraid to move in new directions. During his break he spent some time in New York recording new songs with Full Force, the producers responsible for Backstreet Boys' tune 'All I Have To Give', as well as hits with other groups such as Allure and artists like Samantha Fox and Lisa Lisa.

He also made two trips to Atlanta, Georgia to work with a writer named Gary Baker, who previously penned Backstreet's 'Anywhere For You'. Howie hopes that one of the songs he has helped to write will end up on Backstreet Boys' third album.

Howie would also love to sing more leads on their next CD. In a few live appearances during Brian's period of recuperation from heart surgery, he filled in with the lead on 'Quit Playin' Games (With My Heart)'. He'll admit he was very nervous, but everyone agrees that he did a wonderful job.

But Backstreet Boys isn't the only project he's been working on recently. Partly to repay the debt he owes his sister Polly Anna for being so loving and supportive through the years, Howie is helping his older sister to cut a demo tape of her own music. He describes her sound as a cross between Celine Dion and

Gloria Estefan and hopes that her talents will win her a recording contract.

A skilled businessman, Howie is also starting his own company with members of his family to invest some of the money he's made with Backstreet Boys in property. One of those projects is a block of apartments he's having built on the waterfront in Orlando which he plans to make his permanent residence.

There are also a few more challenges on Howie's horizon.

Although his first love remains singing and dancing, he hasn't forgotten the fun of acting.

He'd love to do some work as an actor in the future. Howie would also enjoy the challenge of going back to college. (He already has a two-year Associate's Degree in the arts.) Howie would also love to become proficient enough at playing the guitar to be able to play with Backstreet Boys in the future. Most of all, he'd like to continue to bring a little bit of Backstreet Boys into people's lives all around the world.

'We have fans of all ages, all races, all sexes,' he reasoned. 'Hopefully we can move people with our music and bring some happiness into other people's lives. Just turn on the radio in your car and listen to our songs and have them move you. Just listen to the music and let it speak for itself.'

HOWIE'S CONFIDENTIAL SECRETS

Howie doesn't like team sports much. He prefers to waterski or play racquetball.

HOWIE RECENTLY INDULGED IN THE ULTIMATE SPORTY CAR – A NEW CHEVROLET CORVETTE.

His favourite trashy thrill is watching the antics of the guests on the Jerry Springer Show.

Of all the guys, it takes Howie the longest to get dressed. He's very finicky about his clothing.

Like Brian, Howie has a phobia about heights.

He cried while watching the movie 'Titanic'.

No matter how tired he is at night, Howie never goes to bed without doing his stomach-crunch exercises.

He was such a huge Michael Jackson fan that as a youngster he even rode a 'Thriller' skateboard!

HE RECENTLY BOUGHT A LAPTOP COMPUTER THAT HE TAKES WITH HIM ON THE ROAD.

Howie once worked as a tour guide at Universal Studios in Orlando.

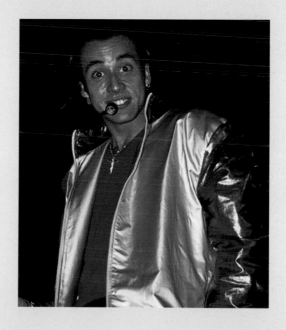

Chapter Seven

Backstreet Boys in Concert

ONE OF THE THINGS THAT DISTINGUISHES BACKSTREET BOYS FROM ALL OTHER VOCAL GROUPS IS THEIR LIVE SHOW. WITH CHOREOGRAPHY, COSTUMES, LIGHTING AND SPECIAL EFFECTS THAT WOULD OUTSHINE THE AVERAGE BROADWAY MUSICAL, AND EXCITING LIVE RENDITIONS OF THE SONGS THAT FANS WANT TO HEAR MOST, IT'S A TREAT FOR EARS AND EYES ALIKE.

BACKSTREET Boys don't just recreate their videos on stage; they get the audience involved. The guys love the moment when the houselights come up to reveal everyone dancing and singing along in the audience. Such moments are what the members of Backstreet live for. It's their goal to make sure that their fans have as much fun in the audience as they're having on stage. And clearly, Backstreet Boys are having the time of their lives!

'When you're a singer on stage, of course, you can see the reaction of the people,' explained Kevin. 'That is the greatest feeling of all. That's what we're here for. That's a natural high to have people cheering.'

Backstreet Boys are proud of their live performances. They give 100 per cent towards creating a uniquely memorable concert experience. 'You go to see certain groups and they may just stand there and sing or they may move a little bit,' AJ said. 'We just try to put on a good show and give the people what they came to see.'

The 1998 Backstreet Boys show, which toured all over Europe and Canada, and finally reached the United States in July, was the most ambitious show that the group had staged to date. The guys made their entrance accompanied by a fireworks display that left no doubt that everyone was in for a good time. The performance highlighted all of the hits their fans wanted to hear including 'Quit Playin' Games (With My Heart)', 'As Long As You Love Me', 'Everybody (Backstreet's

Back)', 'I'll Never Break Your Heart', 'All I Have To Give' and 'We've Got It Goin' On'.

Many fans find the group members' solo sets to be the high point of the show as well as the most personal moment, as each Backstreet Boy is given free rein to choose his own songs. For American audiences, it was also the opportunity to hear some of the tunes from the group's debut European album and the follow-up *Backstreet's Back* that weren't included on their American release. Nick's solo included two songs not released in America, 'Party' and 'Heaven In Your Eyes', while Howie's choice was 'My Heart Stays With You', a song written and produced by Full Force. Kevin's moment in the spotlight featured another song new to the US, 'Nobody But You', which he also premiered all over Europe earlier in the year. AJ, meanwhile, chose the B-side to 'Quit Playin' Games (With My Heart)' a romantic tune called 'If You Lay Down'. Finally, Brian sang the song he helped write on *Backstreet's Back*, the heartfelt 'That's What She Said'.

'When you're a singer on stage, of course, you can see the reaction of the people.'

Backstreet Boys' inventive choreography was displayed to great effect on the 1998 tour. The chair routine, which flows so smoothly it has to be seen to be believed, is revived from their video during 'As Long As You Love Me'. Backstreet Boys also became the Hat Squad for the song 'All I Have To Give', a fan favourite during which the Boys wear, pass and flip their fedoras fluidly in unison. Although they make it look easy, Nick has pointed out that a lot of hard work goes into a Backstreet Boys routine.

'We don't really have much rehearsal for the singing because we do it all the time, but choreography-wise, we rehearse our butts off!'

The lady responsible for putting Backstreet Boys through their dance paces and creating most of their unique choreography is Fatima Robinson. She's been with Backstreet Boys since the beginning and the guys have nothing but praise for her skill, patience and innovation. 'She did a lot of work with Michael Jackson, Brandy and Bobby Brown,' explained Howie. 'We feel comfortable with her style because she realizes we do a lot of singing – live vocals. You can't do too much jumping because you're constantly singing. So she creates good moves [for us], that look really flashy.'

Although at this point in their careers, dancing and singing are the focus of a Backstreet Boys show, the group did take over from their six-piece backing band to perform a unique version of 'Quit Playin' Games (With My Heart)'. With Howie on lead guitar, AJ on bass, Nick pounding the drums, Kevin commandeering the keyboards and Brian creating some percussion on the bongos, it may have been a preview of the Backstreet Boys of the future.

For AJ and the rest of Backstreet Boys, performing live is a way to prove to the sceptics that Backstreet Boys are not just a 'boy band' with more looks than talent. 'Some people look at us, and of course, they are a little sceptical because

they see New Kids or New Edition, but then they hear us sing live and they step back and they kind of go "Wow! These guys are real, these guys are doing something that they love and you can see it written all over them,"' he said.

Behind The Scenes

Every performer has his own little backstage ritual before a show and the members of Backstreet Boys are no exception. Howie has his tea with lemon to prime his vocal chords for the workout to come. Kevin avoids dairy products,

which can compromise the clarity of his voice. Nick and Brian rev up with soft drinks – the kind with sugar and caffeine in them – so that they're laughing and bouncing off the walls of their dressing room before a show. AJ spends an enormous time with his hair and clothing stylists plotting ways to make himself stand out – as if he could ever just melt into the background!

The final preparations for the show begin hours before the group goes on when they arrive with the band for a sound check. The feeling is casual as they

pace the stage, stand in front of different lighting effects and just get comfortable with the feel of a new venue. Although Backstreet carries its own equipment from city to city, each venue from an 8,000 seat arena to an outdoor stadium with a 19,000 seat capacity has subtle differences and it's important that the group gets a good idea of how much room they have to work with. But boys will always be boys! After the check is done, they often can't resist the urge to pick up the band's instruments and jam for a while.

Depending on how much time there is before the show, they might go back to their hotel for dinner. Other times, a catered supper is brought in for the whole crew which often includes the band, tour managers, road crew and stylists. All the members of the group try to eat healthily on the road. Even AJ, with his famous fondness for McDonald's quarter pounders with cheese, loads up on pasta, salads and fresh fruit on the night of a show. 'You find that [if] you eat the wrong things you get run down quicker,' he said. On tour 'I want to be on a stricter diet, try to build up a little and eat a lot healthier and drink a lot of water to keep my stamina up'. Despite all the healthy resolutions, if there's chocolate anything being served for dessert, count on all five members of Backstreet Boys to go up for seconds on the sweets!

Finally the group retires to the dressing room to get ready for the show. The 1998 personal stylist and makeup person, Angela Lehman, has said that keeping up with Backstreet Boys is a challenge! For starters, AJ's hairstyling needs changing daily. Over the course of one summer he dyed his hair red with blond streaks, picked it out into an afro, added dreadlock extensions, dyed it platinum and then finally shaved it all off! Brian and Nick, meanwhile, like to hold off hair and makeup until the very

last second. They tend to practise basketball shots until they have to be practically dragged to the makeup chair. Howie, however, presents a different problem. He has a tendency to rip the buttons off his shirt during a concert to show off his great upper body. Angela and her assistant once fastened all his buttons with safety pins in an attempt to keep them in place, but the plan backfired when Howie had difficulty making a quick costume change! Finally, there's Kevin who, she admits, is never any trouble at all!

One of Backstreet Boys' rituals is that they all share one dressing room prior to the show. As they put on their costumes, have their hair styled and make up applied, they mentally walk through the show and discuss any adjustments they need to make. Although Backstreet Boys make it all look so easy on stage, they are always trying to improve their performances.

They pay serious attention to the advice of the people in their organization, and Backstreet Boys also carefully go over the reviews printed in the popular press. 'We are always looking and reading through a lot of magazines that have articles on us,' explained Howie. 'We know that not everyone is going to like Backstreet Boys. Like critics. There are going to be some who accept us for who we are, and there are going to be some

Although Backstreet Boys make it all look so easy on stage, they are always trying to improve their performances.

who want us to be something we are not. We always take things for what they are worth, and sometimes we use some things for motivation and positive criticism, then we can help ourselves become better.'

Before a show, the group also takes time to warm up both physically, with lots of stretches, and vocally, with some a cappella singing. It's a ritual they try never to forget to practise, because, they admit, the few times they didn't warm up they were all really sore the day after the show.

The final moment before Backstreet Boys take the stage is reserved for a group prayer. 'Before every show we always hold hands and say a prayer and do a little meditation focus-type thing, all of us,' explained Brian. 'We get together with our security and our tight family out there and we thank God for giving us the talent and for a good show,' added Howie.

'We pray for safety,' Brian said. 'We pray for the audience, so no one gets hurt. It's more or less a focusing point at the beginning to all come together.'

Adds AJ, 'Having a group prayer before each show just allows us to focus and just be one as a whole, instead of five individuals which we are on an everyday basis.'

That Crazy Night

Like any live performance, anything can happen at a Backstreet Boys concert. Over the years and countless shows there have been slip-ups and missed lines, power failures and torn costumes. There have also been lots of funny situations that have caused the guys to lose their cool and burst out laughing. 'If somebody falls down it's funny. If someone falls off the stage, it's not funny,' Kevin said.

Of course there are exceptions.

Everyone can laugh now because no harm was done at the time that Howie flew from the stage and landed on one of the security guards in the pit. It's now a well-remembered bit of Backstreet Boys legend. 'It was an accident, but I

pushed him,' recalled Nick of the fateful night.

'It was absolutely hilarious the way it happened,' said AJ 'Nick opened up his arms like a bird and wasn't paying attention. Howie just happened to walk

'It was an accident, but I pushed him,' recalled Nick of the fateful night.

up behind him and he [Nick] just knocked him off the stage. Our security guard caught him and cushioned his fall. It was just so funny because you look over and there's Howie, and then you look over, and he's gone! Like, where'd he go? You look down and he's in the pit, like, "hi guys!"'

Another hazard is fans throwing things – even with the best intentions – up on stage. At a show in Europe a fan threw a pack of cigarettes which Kevin slipped on. Fortunately, he wasn't hurt. 'I don't even know if anybody noticed,' he said. 'It was a move that sort of ... we're all spinning around and we go down really low. I just spun around and hit the floor and got up.'

Poor Kevin! He may have got away with it that night, but an entire club audience probably noticed the time he split his trousers on stage during one show early in the history of Backstreet Boys. 'I was in black overalls and they

were really baggy but they looked cool,' he recalled. 'We were on stage and we were doing our number called "Get Down". All of a sudden there's a part where we go, *"and I want it right now,"* and I go RRRRRIPPPPPPP! My pants ripped right open!' Of course Kevin, a firm believer in the old maxim 'the show must go on,' finished the routine before he went backstage to change.

There have been other memorable incidents too. The guys recall one night when power was lost on the monitors and the band's equipment during Howie's solo. 'We blew the power out on stage and Howie was all by himself singing,' recalled Brian. 'The whole band was jamming, he's dancing and singing, and we're in the back changing...' 'And everything goes out except his mike,' continued Kevin. With his microphone still working, Sweet D saved the day by singing *a cappella* until the problem could be solved.

At another show, this time in Germany, AJ accidentally threw the sports jersey he was wearing on a hot stage light during a quick costume change. Luckily, manager Johnny Wright smelled something burning backstage and removed the scorched shirt before the fire brigade had to be called. Brian's still slightly annoyed at the memory because the jersey that AJ was wearing that night was his!

Even old pros like Backstreet Boys can sometimes forget the lyrics or the dance steps to a song.

Brian recalled that the most embarrassing thing that's ever happened to him on stage was the time he got too enthusiastic during a choreographed move and kicked his shoe off. He hopped around with only one shoe on until Kevin was able to cross the stage and bring it back for him!

The group's microphones, at times, haven't turned off when they've gone backstage – allowing the audience to hear everything the guys have said. 'That's happened a couple of times. There have been times where Howie's on stage and all four of us are in the back getting changed and we're all talking and Howie's singing. We're all going, "I can't believe the Bulls [Chicago basketball team] lost!" And it's coming through the monitors!' recalled AJ. 'Howie's probably going, "Shut up, you idiots!"'

Even old pros like Backstreet Boys can sometimes forget the lyrics or the dance steps to a song. Brian remembered a night where AJ said something funny and suddenly his mind went totally blank. 'I don't actually remember what he said. But I happened to look back at him and I started laughing,' recalled Brian. 'I was supposed to be singing and I was like, "What am I supposed to sing?" The verse started and I was going "Da, da, da, da, da."'

While silly mishaps and funny moments can happen on any night of a Backstreet Boys show (though they try their best to avoid them), on the last night of a tour something will definitely happen! It's become a tradition. Starting with their very first excursion across the United States playing high schools, Backstreet Boys, their crew and their management have delighted in playing increasingly inventive practical jokes on

each other during the last show of the tour, which they've christened 'The Crazy Night'.

Most of the jokes are played on the group. On one tour in the Christmas season Backstreet Boys were wearing Santa robes while singing *a cappella*. During the number, an enormous twelve-foot-tall decorated tree was supposed to descend from the lighting rig behind the group. On the last night of the tour, the crew switched to a small one-and-a-half-foot tree decorated with just a handful of lights. Echoing a very funny moment from the movie *This Is Spinal Tap*, it descended from the ceiling and hung right over the Boys, often hitting them in the heads as they sang. The crew was in hysterics and Backstreet Boys, to their credit, carried on like there was nothing wrong!

Another time the crew decided those Backstreet Boys needed more fibre in their diets. 'We did "Boys Will Be Boys" and we were supposed to dance with our mike stands,' recalled AJ 'They put carrots in the mike stands. I didn't know what it was and I just couldn't stop laughing'.

Of course, this group is pretty good at playing their own tricks too. AJ once filled the drummer's hat with Cheerios causing a rain of bits of dry cereal when the poor man put it on! The group's introduction of the band to the audience is frequently laced with funny noises and new nicknames on The Crazy Night, too. 'Anything can happen on the last show,' said Howie.

Whether the night is crazy or not, every performance is something special for the members of the group.

'They put carrots in the mike stands. I didn't know what it was and I just couldn't stop laughing.'

Chapter Eight

AJ McLean Confidential

'Nothing embarrasses me – I'm pretty goofy.'

AJ IS THE MEMBER OF BACKSTREET BOYS MOST LIKELY TO KEEP HIS FANS GUESSING. FROM HIS CLOTHES TO HIS HAIRSTYLES TO THE SPONTANEOUS DANCE MOVES HE'LL DO ON STAGE, LIFE IS ALWAYS AN ADVENTURE FOR THIS MOST UNPREDICTABLE STAR.

the bed and I guess the cleaning lady came in and thought it was a rag. It looked like one. It was gone when I came back,' he has said. 'The day I was born I was wrapped in this thing. My great-grandmother made it for me.'

ALEXANDER James McLean was born on 9 January 1978 at Bethesda Memorial Hospital in Palm Beach, Florida. His father Robert worked with computers for IBM, while his mother Denise was employed at a local hotel. Although his parents divorced when he was just four years old, that didn't stop AJ from having a wonderful childhood. By his own admission, he was spoiled rotten by his mum! He also maintained friendly relations with his dad who he says is proud of his son, the star.

AJ has the benefit of a large and loving extended family, too. Although he's an only child, his grandparents, aunts, uncles and cousins have always admired his talent and been supportive of his dreams. Today, they're all practically crowing with pride. 'My grandparents are very supportive. My grandmother idolizes me. She's the sweetest lady in the world,' he's said. 'My Uncle Bill and Aunt Darlene, my cousin Kathy – these are my closest relatives and they are all so supportive. They always try to come out and see a show.'

Family ties mean everything to AJ, who's sentimental to the core. Over his years with Backstreet Boys, he's repeated to journalists all over the world the story of the fateful day he lost his 'blankie' in a hotel room in North Carolina on BSB's first tour of North America. 'I left it in

All through school, most of AJ's closest friends were female. He admits that he often prefers the company of women to men. This smooth charmer has the power to coax even the shyest girl to self-revelation. And, when AJ likes someone on a romantic level – look out! He's the most romantic, flirtatious, thoughtful guy in the group. 'I was raised in a feminine household,' he reasoned, 'and I was raised to treat women with respect.'

Credit for AJ's enlightened views of women goes to his mother Denise, who's also one of his closest friends. As a child, she encouraged him to take classes in all the things he loved – singing, dancing and acting. She drove him to auditions and cheered for him in talent competitions. In short, AJ would never have been so successful in his life without her!

Today, although AJ is grown up, he and his mother remain extremely close. When he joined Backstreet Boys, he was still a minor so his mum was legally required to travel with him on tour. Not the sort of person who enjoys just sitting

around, Denise started helping the group out by ironing their stage clothes and helping them find their shoes in the wardrobe department. She also pitched in selling T-shirts and cassettes and doing anything else she could think of to help. When AJ turned eighteen, Denise took a job working in the offices of the group's management company in Orlando. These days she's Backstreet Boys' personal publicity contact, handling all the press requests that the group receives on the road. AJ, who always felt so bad about leaving Denise at home while he travelled

the world, is thrilled to have her along. Their time off is often spent together shopping or going to late-night movies.

When AJ's not working or shopping, he can often be found talking to one of his millions of friends on the phone. He can talk anyone's ear off! Some lesser known facts about AJ are that he likes to bake biscuits, he's afraid of insects and snakes and he failed the written part of his driver's test more than once! Once he did get his licence, AJ indulged in a really great car. Right now, he's driving a blue Mercedes saloon, which he absolutely adores. On the sports front, AJ enjoys basketball, billiards and playing golf. His favourite holidays are Halloween, because he loves dressing in costumes, and St. Valentine's Day, because he's romantic to the core!

Family ties mean everything to AJ, who's sentimental to the core.

In The Beginning

Energetic AJ discovered the limelight very early in his life. At five, he started modelling for JC Penny's department store catalogues. He took a huge step forward in the show business hierarchy when a director for the local Royal Palm Dinner Theatre spotted him and invited Denise to bring AJ to audition. His first theatrical role was playing Dopey in a production of *Snow White and the Seven Dwarves*. AJ says he stole the show with his antics even though he didn't have any lines! Over the course of the next two years this feisty kid would appear in 27 plays.

At the age of twelve, AJ and his mother moved to

Orlando to enrol him in a performing arts school. His studies included classes in singing and acting, but his favourite lessons were in dance. 'Tap, jazz, ballet, hip-hop, gymnastics – you name it, I've done it', he says today. That training shows up in AJ's ability to pick up new

dance steps faster than all the other Boys. As they visit the hottest dance spots all over the world, he, Howie and Kevin are always on the lookout for new moves. 'We go out to the clubs and we do the latest moves and the latest fads', he says. Having already seen or tried a new move casually on a London or New York dance floor makes it easier for Backstreet's choreographer Fatima Robinson to incorporate new material into their show.

Though he loves dance, AJ was pretty passionate about acting as a kid, too. He spent the hours after classes making the rounds of auditions and was rewarded with several television roles. One of his early successes was a part in the Nickelodeon series *Hi Honey, I'm Home*, which may be the root cause of AJ's flirtation with ever-changing hairstyles. To play the character Skunk in the syndicated series, AJ had his hair shaved into a Mohawk cut and bleached yellow! Additionally, AJ worked as an extra on the series *Welcome Freshman* and *Fifteen*. Although he tried out for *The Mickey Mouse Club*, he never became a regular performer on that show.

Once AJ had his hair shaved into a Mohawk cut and bleached yellow!

Alone in his room as a child, surrounded by soft toys, AJ nurtured a vivid fantasy life that stimulated his interest in puppets. 'I was bored. I used to have a lot of plush toys and I'd play with the plush toys and I got into puppets,' he explained. 'I did a lot of talent shows with ... puppets. It just caught on because no one had seen anyone my age be that interested and having that much fun doing stuff with puppets. I got a major kick out of it and I still do.'

When AJ looks back now, he has to laugh. He expected to make a career out of everything but singing! 'I wanted to be a dancer or an actor. I wanted it to be my first career,' he has said. 'I never really wanted to be a singer, but it just kind of went that way, I guess.'

Naturally, AJ has no regrets about joining Backstreet Boys. He's even found a valuable outlet for his acting skills during live performances and making music videos. 'It's the best of both worlds,' he said. 'I mean, on stage it's just like acting. You're acting to make the girls swoon. It's the same thing for the cameras. Whenever you're before the cameras, it's acting. You're playing, whether it's with just your eyes and your lips or your face. You're playing out to the crowd in TV land. I'm very happy to be doing everything I ever wanted to do in one shot.'

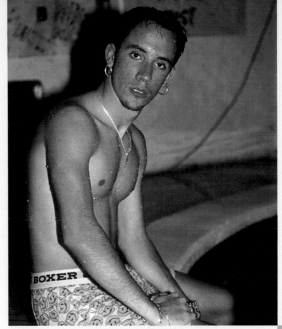

the time of his life decorating and is rumoured to be a daily shopper at the national linen and houseware chain, Bed, Bath and Beyond.

Even-tempered AJ admits that one of the only things he tends to get into an argument about with the other group members is clothes. 'It's always about the stupidest stuff, like what you're going to wear to the show or if one of us buys a

shirt and I buy the same shirt. It's like, "oh, why did you buy that shirt? It's mine,"' he recalled with a laugh.

Armed with the knowledge of how fussy AJ is about his wardrobe, the other guys have targeted him as an easy mark for practical jokes. On one tour early in their careers, Nick, Kevin and Brian stole all of AJ's clothes from his unlocked hotel room. They quite enjoyed watching poor AJ run about screaming that he'd been robbed! Only when he went to call the hotel's concierge desk did they confess to their crime. More recently, the Boys, who had all agreed to appear dressed in white at a show, hid AJ's black shirt. They knew from experience that he would try to wear the exact opposite. Frantic, AJ finally found his black shirt just before he went on, only to find the other members of the group standing on stage wearing black shirts too.

AKA Bone

Apart from being Backstreet Boys' most agile member, AJ also brings his own irrepressible style to the fold. From fuzzy fake-fur-covered camouflage pants that he tracked down in London's Soho to the long dreadlocks he had weaved into his hair for a Backstreet Boys' benefit performance in Orlando. AJ is the one member of the group who isn't afraid to stand alone.

'I shop more than most women,' he said. In fact, on a perfect day off work, he'd 'shop until I couldn't fit any more bags in my car.' Some of AJ's favourite things to indulge in on a shopping expedition are silver jewellery ('Especially exotic Brazilian types!'), funky club clothes, sports jerseys and, lately, household items!

Huh? Well, during Backstreet's break in the spring of 1998, AJ bought himself a home in the Orlando area. He's having

AJ IS THE ONE MEMBER OF THE GROUP WHO ISN'T AFRAID TO STAND ALONE.

'We act like a bunch of little kids,' AJ said. 'We are like brothers.'

AJ's brothers within the Backstreet Boys organization have christened him with an unusual nickname, Bone. 'Yeah, because basically he's a bone. He's so skinny,' explained Nick. The actual cause of the nickname was a chunky wooden necklace that AJ used to wear that Lonnie Jones, Backstreet's head security guard, claimed looked like a string of bones around his neck. 'I used to wear a lot of beaded jewellery, like wooden jewellery, and so that's where I got the name from,' AJ said. 'Our chief of security started calling me Bones. We took the "s" off and now they call me Bone all the time. They don't even call me AJ!'

Like the other members of the group, AJ has begun writing songs in preparation for their third CD release. Accustomed to setting his feelings to poetry, the transformation from poet to songwriter has been smooth for AJ. 'I've written about 75 poems between when I was about 15 and now. Coming from a person my age, a lot of what you write is about past experiences,' he reveals.

Maybe not good stuff, but it's always good to write what you feel inside. It helps a lot when we write songs because a lot of my poetry becomes a song.' AJ's favourite poets include T.S. Eliot, Shakespeare and Edgar Allen Poe, although he doesn't predict that too much of their influence will creep into his own work. 'The kind of stuff I write, kids my age or younger can read and understand, because I don't want kids to be reading "for art thous" in my songs.'

'I'm single now so I can write a lot about my past relationships.'

Though he loves his work and the wealth of experience he's gained as a member of Backstreet Boys, he gets a little wistful when he thinks of what it would be like to be a 'normal' person. 'I love being a Backstreet Boy, but I'd trade it all in tomorrow for reality. To step aside from a world like this which is a movie magical world. It's a fantasy world,' he said thoughtfully. 'I mean, this is what I would want to do, step back into reality and be normal again, because this is not really normal. You know, lights, cameras – it's not normal. To people like us it is, but I'd rather be a normal kid playing b-ball and writing music still.'

In an effort to reclaim just a little bit of his life before Backstreet Boys, AJ flew back to Orlando in 1996 to attend his high-school graduation ceremony. Although he spent all of his high school years on the road with a tutor, he still had a lot of friends among the graduates. As a member of Backstreet Boys he's had the opportunity to attend many glamorous awards ceremonies all over the world, but his high school graduation was special in its own right.

AJ would like to see Backstreet Boys become 'one of the most well-rounded and most respectable and influential groups of the time. To never break-up and to never screw-up. To just be real and to prove to people that we can still be in this business and not lose your mind.'

AJ'S CONFIDENTIAL SECRETS

IF AJ HADN'T MADE IT IN SHOW BUSINESS, HE WOULD HAVE LIKED TO STUDY PSYCHOLOGY.

As a youngster, AJ had a speech impediment. He used to lisp and stutter sometimes.

His favourite colour is yellow.

AJ carries his own pillow with him on tour.

His 1998 New Year's resolution was to eat less McDonald's food. He broke that one!

AJ loves sunglasses. He owns many pairs – from cheap ones he's bought at flea market for $5 all the way up to designer shades.

He sometimes wears coloured contact lenses to change his brown eyes to blue – or purple!

HIS ALL-TIME FAVOURITE BACKSTREET BOYS SONG IS '10,000 PROMISES'.

Chapter Nine

As Long As You Love Me

I'm dating, but I don't have anybody serious.'

DO THE MEMBERS OF BACKSTREET BOYS HAVE GIRLFRIENDS? IT'S A QUESTION THEY'RE ASKED BY THE PRESS AND THEIR FANS ALL OVER THE WORLD. THE ANSWER IS USUALLY AN EMPHATIC NO!

T'S a little hard. You kind of get things going and then you've got to leave for two or three months. So you have relationships in spurts,' explained AJ. 'You don't have a full year to be with somebody. It's really difficult to try to maintain a decent relationship, especially when you're a person like me that wants to give either all or nothing. I'm dating, but I don't have anybody serious.'

AJ's sentiments are repeated by all the members of the group, from Howie and Kevin, who say that their romances never progress much past dating, to Brian, who saw a relationship with a girl back home end by mutual consent, to Nick, who adds that he's never actually been in love. 'You don't really have that much time to actually put that much effort into [a relationship],' he has said.

However, all the members of the group confess that they do appreciate women who share their interests and can deal with their hectic schedules.

Nick: The Dreamer

If Nick Carter could have a dinner date with anyone in the world, he'd choose film actress Christina Ricci because 'she's fine as heck'. Like a lot of guys, he also thinks that supermodel Cindy Crawford and actress Sharon Stone are lovely ladies.

Nick, an Aquarian, is a true Florida boy (even if he was born in New York State). He loves women who enjoy the sun and sand as much as he does. A skilled scuba diver, waterskier, fisherman and boater, he spends as much of his free time on the water as possible. One of his favourite ways to treat a special girl is to take her out on his new boat to drift on the ocean under a night sky filled with stars.

This free spirit (another characteristic he gets from his star sign) enjoys the company of girls who are open to spontaneous suggestions. He has so much of his life planned for him as a member of Backstreet Boys that he likes just to float with the wind on his own time.

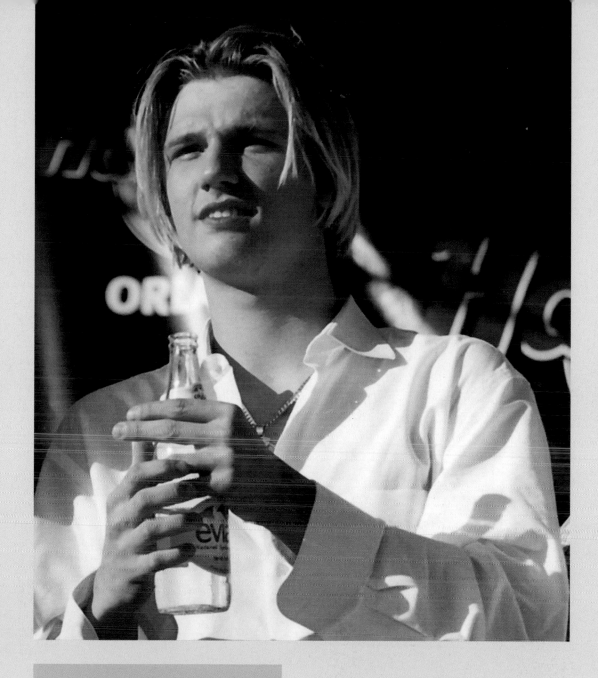

He enjoys midnight movies, video arcade games and long walks on the beach. Although he admits that it would be very inconvenient to fall in love right now, Nick looks forward to the day when he'll have the time to seek out a relationship with someone special who loves him for who he is inside, not because he's a member of Backstreet Boys.

Shared interests and 'a lot of personality' are the qualities he looks for in a love match.

Brian: Long-Distance Lover

When asked to predict which of the group would be the first to get married, Backstreet Boys' vote is split between cousins Kevin and Brian. Kevin received some votes because of his age and the well-known fact that he can hardly wait for the day he can have a family of his own. Brian, meanwhile, is the Backstreet Boy who is best at maintaining long-distance relationships. Although he was quite good about keeping it quiet, he did have a relationship with a girl back home for quite a while. He wrote the song 'That's What She Said' about it.

'We meet girls everywhere but it's hard to spend the time to really get to know someone', he said. 'I had someone at home but – it was just a mutual thing. It's just tough. I'm never home, [so it's] better as a friendship.'

Brian admits that he's happiest when he has a steady love in his life. It fits with his Piscean nature, which makes him shy away from exposing all his deepest, most personal feelings to the new people he meets. Although he's the object of millions of young women's infatuation, he has said that, sadly, that doesn't fulfil his need to have someone just a phone call away who already understands what's in his heart.

People born under the sign of the fish, like Brian, are dreamers who tend

'We meet girls everywhere but it's hard to spend the time to really get to know someone.'

toward sweeping romantic gestures, like a gift of a bouquet of flowers for no reason at all. Good-natured Brian has said that he likes a woman who has 'a great personality, [who's] very open, trusting, giving and just willing to have fun'. He has a mild crush on former *Baywatch* babe Pamela Anderson, though he's yet to meet her.

The Internet was buzzing with rumours recently that Brian is dating Los Angeles actress Leighanne Wallace, who first appeared with Backstreet Boys in the video for 'As Long As You Love Me'. Leighanne is a pretty blonde native of Atlanta, Georgia with her own link to teen stardom – she played Tanna Stewart in the 1997 film *Wild America* starring teen dream Jonathan Taylor Thomas. Leighanne also appeared opposite Brian in the video for 'I'll Never Break Your Heart'. Are they friends or something more? Well, you be the judge because Backstreet Boys aren't talking!

AJ: The Flirt

Jealous girls need not apply to AJ as candidates for a love match! This self-professed lover of women has female friends all over the world. A chronic flirt, AJ just can't help turning on the charm to anyone who comes into his circle.

Although it's been a while since he had more than just casual dates, AJ has said that he likes to put all of his energies into maintaining romance. He's the most likely to appear under a girl's window one night to serenade her with a song or to present a special someone with a little gift to remember him by when he leaves on tour. 'I'm the type of guy that likes to be there almost 24/7 [24 hours a day, 7 days a week],' he says. 'I'm Mr Roses. I'm as old-fashioned as they come. Even though I'm a flirt and I'll talk to girls a lot, if I were to pick one girl, I'd try to give her as much time and respect as I could. That's why if I can't give her all the time that she would want, it's not worth it. It's either all or nothing for me.'

Generous AJ has the ability to charm ladies of all ages. Backstreet's manager Donna Wright recalled a recent Mother's Day when he gave her a present of a guardian angel pin for all the years she's looked after the group. It was a sweet thought and a gift she won't soon forget.

It's AJ's hope that the message of what a wonderful guy he is reaches the ears of No Doubt's lead singer Gwen

Stefani. He's got a mad crush on her! In fact, at the 1997 MTV Europe Awards, AJ cast a silent spell that her boyfriend Gavin Rossdale of Bush would lose in his band's bid for best rock act. Maybe it worked! The award went to Oasis.

AJ's kind of girl is 'someone that has a really catchy personality and is very spontaneous,' he has said. Someone who 'doesn't care wherever we go. We can just go to McDonald's and she'd still have a good time. Just a person who has a lot of good morals inside and is very personable.'

This fun-loving Capricorn has a vivid fantasy date he'd love to make reality one day. Picture a starry night and a young couple walking together on a windswept beach. 'I'd love to have a little sand fight on the beach and throw water at each other,' he imagined. 'Then, I'd serenade her and buy her ice cream.'

'I'm as old-fashioned as they come.'

Howie: Latin Lover

Loyal, reliable, personable Howie was born under the sign of Leo, the lion. An unrepentant 'people person', Howie has a tendency to make friends wherever he goes. No matter what the circumstances, he'll always find some common ground with anyone he is introduced to.

Although he's yet to meet her, Howie would love the opportunity to take supermodel Cindy Crawford out for dinner! He saw her in California recently, but didn't get the opportunity to say hello. 'I don't mind older women', he said with a laugh.

Luckily, Howie also enjoys the company of women who are mere mortals too. Ladies who enjoy dancing, good conversation, and who aren't embarrassed by romantic gestures are perfect matches for Howie. He also thinks girls who are a little shy are sort of sexy.

Pressed for the details of his most romantic display, Howie recalled the birthday surprise he planned for an ex-girlfriend several years ago. 'I asked her parents if I could cook at the house. I cooked a grilled dinner and had a candlelight little thing,' he remembered. 'We ended up going from there over to the airport. There's a strip right near the runway where you can watch the planes take off. I had a sunroof and we just watched the planes go by.'

Kevin: Husband Material!

Kevin's just as ambitious in his approach to romance as he is about Backstreet Boys. He's had serious relationships in the past – he was even engaged to be married at the age of nineteen – but the business of Backstreet Boys takes top priority in his life now. He has, however, promised himself that he will slow down to create a personal life of his own some day.

Kevin adores children! He relishes the time he spends with his goddaughter Madison. 'Her mom says she wants to marry me when she grows up,' confided Kevin with a grin. Watching Madison grow up has given him a reason for wanting more out of life than just the fame that Backstreet Boys has provided. Kevin has also stood by as many of his old friends in Kentucky have paired up, got married and started families. 'I don't want to be out on the road all my life,' he's said. 'I want to have a family some day. The road life is not an easy thing. I don't think I could manage a family and be the kind of father I need to be travelling out on the road.'

This serious-minded Libra likes women who have brains, are classy and professional. Since he's a little bashful himself, he's drawn to smart, friendly girls who are just as sure of where they're headed in life as he is. Ladies who enjoy music, movies, dancing, sports and the beach are very desirable!

Though he relished clubbing every night during his younger years, Kevin prefers to get to know someone under quieter circumstances these days. A perfect date, according to him, would include 'some dinner [and] good conversation. If the vibe is right maybe a romantic walk in a park or on a beach. Yeah, something like that.'

He's drawn to smart, friendly girls who are just as sure of where they're headed in life as he is.

Chapter Ten

Kevin Richardson
Confidential

ONE OF THE REASONS THAT FANS ALL OVER THE WORLD AND OF EVERY AGE GROUP LOVE BACKSTREET BOYS IS BECAUSE THERE'S SOMEONE FOR EVERYONE. THOSE WHO LIKE THEIR POP STARS TALL, DARK AND HANDSOME NEED LOOK NO FURTHER THAN KEVIN RICHARDSON.

THE eldest of the group is also the most thoughtful, serious and a tad shy – an irresistible combination for the thinking woman. And talking of the Backstreet Boys fans who love Kevin most, woman is the key word here. Many of his fans aren't teenagers. In fact, more than one mother dragged to a Backstreet Boys' concert by her pre-teenage daughter has forgotten her dignity for a moment and joined in the cheers and screams for this green-eyed performer!

Kevin's personal qualities include his zeal for perfection, his dedication to hard work and his quest to make sure that Backstreet Boys remains a viable world-renowned singing group for years to come. Perhaps because he's the oldest, he's often the one who calls group meetings or sounds the alarm to the other members to show that playtime is over and it's time to get down to work. Fearless in his pursuit of his dreams, this usually soft-spoken singer from Kentucky can be quite strident when it comes to defending the legacy of his solid-platinum group. He's not afraid to speak his mind about the future of Backstreet Boys, even when he's talking to the head of his record label. 'I'm a real perfectionist,' he's said many times. 'I want things to be done right.'

Where does Kevin get his drive for perfection? He supposes a lot of it goes back to his childhood growing up as the youngest of three brothers. Kevin Scott Richardson was born on 3 October 1972 to Ann, a housewife, and Jerald, who tried his hand at several careers – from fireman to pharmaceutical salesman to construction worker to the director of a children's summer camp. Kevin's brothers are Jerald Jr and Tim. He admits he grew up closest to Tim because they're only four years apart in age. The two of them, who both played American football and Little League baseball, were quite competitive about athletics. Kevin has also conceded that he's lost more than one would-be girlfriend to his charming older brother.

HE'S NOT AFRAID TO SPEAK HIS MIND ABOUT THE FUTURE OF BACKSTREET BOYS

Kevin has often described his childhood years as idyllic. His earliest memories are of living in Harrodsburg, a small historic town about 45 minutes from Lexington, Kentucky. Although his family were not farmers they grew a variety of vegetables, such as corn, lettuce, beans, and tomatoes, and they even had their own cow. There's a part of Kevin who misses that connection with the land and wonders what it would have been like to become a farmer. The Richardson brothers spent their time riding dirt bikes and horses, running through the woods and helping out around the farm. Kevin has a lot of really happy memories of those years.

Kevin's family moved to Beattyville, a town in the Appalachian Mountains of Kentucky, when he was eight. There, his father ran a summer camp and retreat centre. 'I was fortunate to grow up there,' said Kevin. 'I had tons of friends because every summer the camp was filled with kids my age. I met people from all over the state and sometimes from all over the country as well.'

During the summer, autumn and spring months the camp would be filled with people, but in the winter, Kevin and his family had the entire seventeen-room building to themselves.

Kevin recalled that it was 'sort of like living two different lives'. During termtime, he and his brothers would take a bus to school several miles away in town. He played sports and was very popular with his fellow classmates. In the warmer months, he wouldn't see his school friends because he'd spend all of his time helping his father at the camp

Home was an enormous log cabin on the edge of a cliff overlooking a peaceful valley.

and making friends with all of the new children who came for stays of about two weeks. 'There was no reason to leave at all – all these people coming up to talk to, play with, to meet,' he recalls. '[There were] lots of cute girls. I'd get my heart broken every summer, because I would find a girlfriend and then she would leave and I wouldn't see her again.' Despite frequent teenage heartbreak, it was a very happy time in Kevin's life.

Music also played a very important role in Kevin's upbringing. There was always music in the Richardson family – whether it was on the radio, the record player, at church, or while driving in the car. In fact, Kevin remembered that he first began harmonizing with his mother Ann on long car rides. Kevin's mother was locally famous for her beautiful voice. She sang in church most Sundays and frequently performed at weddings.

As soon as he was old enough, Kevin also joined the youth choir at his church. 'I grew up singing in church,' said Kevin. 'Me and my mom – who is Brian's father's sister – I sang duets with her in church.'

Singing isn't Kevin's only musical talent though. 'Kevin's played piano since he could walk, I think,' fellow Backstreet Boy AJ McLean has joked with admiration. 'He plays by ear. He doesn't read music but he does fantastic arrangements and

[song] writing.' Kevin, however, claims he's no child prodigy. He actually began playing piano at nine years of age. A self-taught musician, he adds that a gift for music runs in his family as his grandfather, grandmother and all their brothers and sisters could play piano by ear. Kevin received his first set of electric

keyboards in his first year at high school. He was soon playing in public every chance he got – at restaurants, wedding and school talent shows.

As a Backstreet Boy, it was one of Kevin's greatest thrills to meet two of his piano-playing idols, Elton John and Billy Joel. 'I've always liked a wide variety of music,' Kevin has said. 'I like the Eagles, Van Halen, Aerosmith, Prince, Elton John, Billy Joel, Boyz II Men, New Edition. All these people had influences on the way I sing and on my love of music.'

Kevin got his first experience of the stage in local productions of the musicals *Bye Bye Birdie* and *Barefoot In The Park*. His natural grace and the ease with which he learned dance routines landed him a job teaching ballroom dancing. But eventually, Lexington proved to be too small a city to hold Kevin's talent.

'I'd get my heart broken every summer, because I would find a girlfriend and then she would leave and I wouldn't see her again.'

It's neither New York nor Los Angeles, but Orlando has quietly earned a reputation as a great city for young people looking for a way to break into the entertainment business. With so many theme parks needing singers, dancers and actors to entertain their tourists, there's plenty of work for talented good-looking people with a flair for performing. Although he's confessed that it was one of the hardest things he'd ever done, Kevin moved to Orlando with the encouragement of his father. He quickly landed a job with Walt Disney World where his dark hair, handsome face and impressive height made him a dead ringer for their cartoon character Aladdin.

Kevin sang at the theme park during the day and appeared as Aladdin at the Disney-MGM Studios theme park daily parade. As night fell, he roamed around Orlando listening to live music in clubs, always on the lookout for an opportunity to promote his own music. He played and DJ'ed at clubs (something he continues to do even now) and talked to anyone who would listen to his dreams. Through the Orlando grapevine, he eventually heard about a young vocal group looking for new members. 'There were two other members who didn't work out and I replaced one of them,' he explained. 'Then, we needed another member...and I called Brian.'

AKA Train

Within Backstreet Boys, Kevin has always assumed the role of group leader. The oldest of the group, he's not as exuberant as notorious pranksters Nick and Brian are. Yes, he has a sense of humour – the cartoon TV show *South Park* can make him convulse with laughter – but not when it comes to Backstreet Boys.

'Kevin is a perfectionist,' his cousin Brian has said. 'He's got a lot of positive aspects, but he lets his perfectionist side get in the way sometimes because he wants things to be too perfect. He knows he needs to lighten up – sometimes he looks at people and they think he's going to rip their heads off.'

A perfectionist on the basketball court as well as the stage, Brian and Nick have nicknamed him 'Train' for his ability to run over the opposition in his bid for the hoop.

Kevin has been the most determined to learn everything he can about the producing side of the recording business. He's never been afraid to ask questions and he's insatiably curious. 'I've learned so much as far as production [is concerned],' he said. 'I mean, I was just soaking all that up like a sponge. It's been a great experience and it's a lot of work.'

Over his years in Backstreet Boys, Kevin has grown personally, too. Although he admits that he has the worst temper in the group, he's learned not to turn its full force on any one member. In times of stress, he turns to Howie, the most easy-going of the five, for a little bit of diplomacy. 'Sometimes, we'll get together and talk to the other guys because he doesn't want to come across as the one telling everyone what to do,' Howie has explained. 'He's mature, responsible, professional and knows what he wants.'

In the earliest years of the group, Kevin and Nick had the most trouble getting along. While Kevin was the mature one, Nick, the group's youngest, liked to play practical jokes or tease the other guys to the breaking point. Tempers flared occasionally. However, these days, Nick has matured and Kevin has learned how to approach him in a manner that doesn't seem like an attack.

Kevin has also learned to allow himself to be vulnerable sometimes. This sensitive guy admits that sometimes it's not hard to make him cry. When he, Nick, Howie and AJ played a show as a foursome at Disney World's annual 'Grad Night' celebration – on the very evening that his cousin Brian was undergoing heart surgery – Kevin wasn't shy about confessing how worried he was. During the group prayer, a couple of tears slid down his face and he allowed the other guys to comfort him. 'It actually hit home a lot with me. I was pretty scared when Brian went into the hospital, because open heart surgery... that's a big thing. Even though technology is great and everything, they say no worries, you know anything can happen,' he said in an interview just weeks after Brian's operation.

'I'M JUST THANKFUL THAT HE MADE IT THROUGH.'

Brian's illness also brought home tragic memories to Kevin of how he lost his father Jerald to cancer of the colon in 1991, when Kevin was 19 years old. It was the first major tragedy in Kevin's life. Today, he keeps the memory of Jerald Richardson alive by carrying a picture of him and of the rest of his family everywhere he roams around the world. He also dedicated Backstreet Boys' debut album to his father's memory. Being a member of Backstreet Boys has been Kevin's proudest achievement, but there is one thing in the world he'd rather have. 'The only [thing] I'd trade it in for is to have my dad back,' he's said.

The Other Side

On the personal front, Kevin is an extremely sweet guy who enjoys shrugging off the role of businessman sometimes and having fun. On the road, Kevin, Howie and AJ often go out clubbing where they can check out the newest dance moves and then take

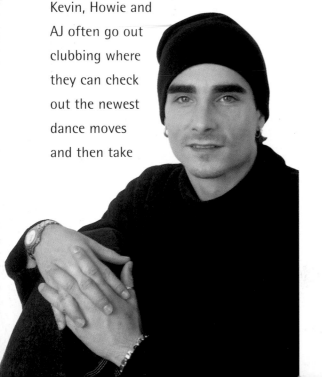

He's a skilled waterskier and surfer

to the floor themselves. Kevin still enjoys playing DJ, so if he's in a city where he knows someone who will let him spin some discs, he's there.

Kevin also enjoys the other benefits his travels around the world have provided. Early on, when Backstreet Boys' fame didn't curtail his activities so much, he loved visiting museums and historic sites en route. He has an adventurous palate and loves sampling the local cuisine in every country he visits. Lately, he much prefers candlelit dinner dates instead of straining to be heard above the noisy throb of a nightclub.

Athletic Kevin enjoys sports too. This transplant to sunny Florida loves lying on the beach and swimming. He's a skilled waterskier and surfer as well. Like his fellow Backstreet Boys, his all-time favourite sport is basketball. He also enjoys playing hockey and American football.

Although he does enjoy shopping sometimes, Kevin's not as excited about material things as some of his fellow Backstreet Boys. He's pretty smart about saving money, but he's also done some extremely generous things – like paying off the mortgage on his mother's home in Kentucky. His three biggest purchases for himself since he's become famous are a house in Florida, a new black Toyota Pathfinder, and an original work of art to decorate his house. 'Finally, I have a place to hang my hat,' he enthused. 'For a while I was living in hotels or staying with friends. Now I have my own place with some friends of mine.'

But Kevin is truly happiest when he's performing with Backstreet Boys or working on songs for their future CDs. Becoming a bona fide songwriter has always been one of his most cherished dreams. He's cut back on his club crawling somewhat these days to spend some quality time with his keyboards. 'I don't go anywhere without my keyboard,' he has said. 'It's good and it's bad because I have to lug that thing around, but I can't be where I'm not able to play – I go through withdrawal!'

For Kevin, watching people all over the world sing along to Backstreet Boys' music is the greatest reward. 'This whole time is like a dream come true,' he said. 'I'm happy to have a job that I love to do. I love to sing. When I was little, I dreamed of singing in front of thousands of people and I'm getting to do it.'

KEVIN'S CONFIDENTIAL SECRETS

As a young man, Kevin seriously considered joining the air force to become a pilot.

If he could have a conversation with anyone, alive or dead, he'd like to chat with Elvis Presley about music.

KEVIN WOULD LOVE TO PRODUCE OR WRITE SONGS FOR OTHER GROUPS SOME DAY.

Kevin pumps weights before he goes on stage with Backstreet Boys.

KEVIN RECENTLY HAD A RECORDING STUDIO INSTALLED IN HIS NEW HOUSE.

Kevin is turned off by women who are really loud, but he appreciates those who are sophisticated and professional.

GOOD LOOKS RUN IN THE RICHARDSON FAMILY. KEVIN'S OLDEST BROTHER JERALD WAS A MODEL AT ONE TIME.

Kevin is the only member of Backstreet Boys who is left-handed.

Chapter Eleven

The Future

WHAT DOES THE FUTURE HOLD FOR BACKSTREET BOYS NOW THAT THEY'VE ACCOMPLISHED SO MANY OF THE THINGS THEY'VE ALWAYS WISHED FOR? MORE MUSIC IS A CERTAINTY FROM THE GROUP, AS THEY'VE ALREADY BEGUN WRITING SONGS FOR THEIR THIRD ALBUM.

IN FACT, it's their hope that their next release will be global, released in Europe, Canada and the United States at the same time. There are also big plans for a Backstreet Boys world tour in 1999, which will take them first to Europe in the winter and then through Southeast Asia, South America, Canada and then back to the United States.

'It's going to be a big one,' promised Nick, who expressed excitement at the prospect of a worldwide stadium-sized tour with more pyrotechnics, grander stages and more seats in the audience.

Although the group has yet to name the new album, they've joked that they'll call it *Backstreet 3: Backstreet's Back Again.* The group predicts that new

material will still be recognizable as Backstreet Boys, but with a broader range than previous efforts. 'We are not going to make any drastic changes yet,' AJ

promised. Fans should expect more lush ballads, sultry R&B sounds and full-tilt dance grooves from it.

While Backstreet Boys plan to continue their collaborations with the producers and writers responsible for many of their previous hits like New York's Full Force ('All I Have To Give') and Sweden's Max Martin and Dennis Pop ('As Long As You Love Me'), they're also looking forward to working with a host of other talented people. Now that Backstreet Boys is a success, the offers just keep flowing in. 'It's pretty incredible,' said Kevin. 'We've just received a couple of demos from the Bee Gees. Barry Gibb actually sent a demo in with his voice on it for us. We're excited about the possibility of doing some work with him.

'There's also a possibility that we're going to be working with Dianne Warren and, let's see, Jermaine Dupris, and maybe, Teddy Riley from BLACKstreet. So we're looking forward to the possibility of working with all these great producers.'

The group has taken to heart some of the critics' complaints that they don't write enough of their own material. It's something they plan to change with their third release. 'As far as critics talking about us not writing our own music, you've got to start from somewhere,' said Kevin defending the group. 'Look at all the other groups like New Edition, Boyz II Men, Madonna, Michael Jackson, Janet – they didn't start out writing their own songs. We've got to start from somewhere and we're going to slowly build. We're not going to rush it. We're going to make sure that when we do put songs of our own on the album that they're good quality songs.'

During their break from performing in the spring of 1998, each of the Boys separately met established writers to pen new songs. Though the group is not about to sacrifice quality for the sake of their egos, each member is very excited about the prospect of getting more personally involved with the writing and production of future material.

'This next album you're going to definitely hear a lot more material originally done [by] us,' promised Howie.

They don't claim to be anything that they're not, but Backstreet Boys have also been discussing the possibility of recording some of the new album's backing music for themselves. It's a very real prospect that's been discussed before. When the group went into the studio to lay down the tune '10,000 Promises' there had been talk of Nick supplying some of the song's percussion and Kevin playing piano on the recording. 'I think I definitely want to bring that up again,' said Nick. 'Maybe we can do that on a different song.'

AJ, for his part, believes there are no limits to what the members of Backstreet Boys can accomplish. They've already learned so much. 'I think it has helped a lot [with] the age differences between the five of us and the experiences we've had,' he said. 'Working with so many producers, different studios around the world, learning how to run a 24-track board, learning how to run an omnidirectional mike, learning how to run a keyboard and how to make your own studio. We've learned so much in so little time. Nick is great with video games so he picks up all the electronic stuff like it's nothing.'

'I'm very excited and I'm very happy, but I'm very nervous because you never know what the future holds and we've worked so very hard all over the world,' said Brian.

How do groups avoid becoming a one-hit wonder? While Backstreet Boys don't claim to have all the answers, they do think they have the right idea about staying true to themselves, respectful to theirs fans, and kind to everyone who's helped them on the way up. 'I think it's all a matter of what you do with the success that you're given,' said Kevin. 'If you take it for granted or you get lazy and you slack off and you don't keep improving, you don't keep growing as a performer and as a songwriter. Your albums don't keep getting better and yes, you will fall off.'

Despite their own star status,

'We've learned so much in so little time.'

such an inspiration. Awed by John's ability to reach both English- and Spanish-speaking audiences, Howie began pushing Backstreet Boys in that direction too. The result is that Backstreet Boys are considering releasing some of their hits in Italian, Dutch and German as well as in Spanish. 'It's kind of cool', said AJ 'It allows the fans to have a little something for that country from us that is kind of a personal thing.'

Whether they're chatting with another recording star or sharing a joke with the fellow who runs the lighting grids at their concerts, Backstreet Boys are always personable, polite and humble. There are no star trips with this group! 'If you get big-headed and you don't treat people good in the industry, and if you don't treat the people around you well

and just take advantage of the situation, then you can fall off', Kevin explained.

One of the charming things about Backstreet Boys is that they have never had a master plan as to what kind of image they wanted to portray. They've always been just themselves. 'We've been looked upon in some parts of the world as the next Beatles or the next Jackson Five', said AJ.

'We don't really look at ourselves that way because we are just normal guys doing something that we love to do.'

Backstreet Boys are humbled in the presence of the people who continue to influence their careers. For Kevin, meeting his favourite performers Elton John, Lionel Richie and Billy Joel was a thrill. Meanwhile Brian, a fan of Boyz II Men, was bold enough to suggest that their Boyz and his Boys should work on a project together some day. If both groups can find concurrent time off, it could happen. Howie, meanwhile, took advantage of a chance meeting with his idol, John Secada, to thank him for being

'We have nothing to hide,' he added. 'There is nothing false about Backstreet Boys, everything is legit. We are a vocal/harmony group. We are not a "boy group or boy band". We want people to know that our first priority is really good music.'

While more outrageous groups with more defined 'personalities' have come and gone, Backstreet Boys have tried to let their music speak for itself. It's a plan that's worked for them around the world and one they expect to continue. 'We want really long-term careers in the business. We don't want to be a flash in the pan,' said Howie. 'We're just trying to take every country in the world and give attention to everybody as much as possible. We feel like as long as we're putting out good music we can be around for a long time.'

Backstreet Boys look to the performers who have been able to change with the times as examples to emulate. 'A perfect example is Michael Jackson's career. I mean, he started off with a young fan base. So did Madonna. So did Janet, but they keep evolving with the times. As the music changed, they changed and they evolved and they kept getting better and kept evolving with the

times. I think it's just what you want to do as an artist,' said Kevin.

On the personal front, none of the group's members doubts that there may come a time when one or two of them will branch off into non-Backstreet Boys activity. That time isn't now, they say, but there's no reason to shut out any possibilities. There's also no reason to believe that a solo project by any

member of the group would prevent him from reuniting for more Backstreet Boys business.

'We may split up and do our own thing. There is a solo artist within each of us,' said AJ 'Not right now, but down the road maybe one of us might branch off, like Howie with the Latin market and Nick with the alternative. The group Backstreet Boys will never break up, we'll always be a group but doing different things at different times.'

Those future projects could include a Backstreet Boys movie or roles for different members in films that have no relation to the group. None of the Boys is opposed to either option, but their schedule is booked for most of 1999. Except for the possibility of filming another group commercial as they did in Germany to advertise a brand of pager, a Backstreet Boys film project is likely to be a long way off.

Nick is one of the most enthusiastic about the prospect of a group movie, along the lines of Spice Girls' *Spice World*. 'We've talked about it a few times and four of us in the group have had the experience,' said Nick. 'So why not do something? This fan of adventure movies, such as the *Predator* and *Aliens* movies

'AS LONG AS WE'RE PUTTING OUT GOOD MUSIC WE CAN BE AROUND FOR A LONG TIME.'

and the darkly eerie *Batman* series, has been working on a Backstreet Boys superhero comic book for the past two years. Nick thinks it has all the elements for a successful live action movie too. 'If you come up with a group and try to make a comic out of them it's got to be good', he's said. 'If not, it's going to be corny'.

Howie, AJ and Kevin have all expressed interest in acting. Howie's open to anything – comedy, drama, or action/adventure. For Kevin's part, he's curious about trying his luck in either a television or movie role. He's very open with regard to the kind of parts he'd like to play. 'Any kind. Villain, comedy, character portrait, whatever', he's said.

'There is a solo artist within each of us.'

AJ, meanwhile, is absolutely sold on playing a villain! And if all his wishes came true, he'd be the bad guy in a movie starring his two favourite actors, Dustin Hoffman and Geena Davis. What attraction does playing the villain hold for him? 'The good guys win but the villains are the ones that everyone likes,' he said. 'That's why I'd like to be the villain.' Such sentiments shouldn't surprise his fans who remember the time

he introduced the opening acts of a Backstreet Boys show in Europe dressed as Batman's arch enemy The Riddler!

But fans will have to be patient. Backstreet Boys playing on the silver screen at the local movie theatre is a long way away. 'I think we want to concentrate on our music and we just want to really give our music 100 percent,' said Howie. Not until later down

the road will we ever start really thinking about that stuff.'

As for the Backstreet Boys' music, there's absolutely no limit to what they expect to accomplish. AJ, for one, can imagine them performing together way into the 21st century! 'We're like brothers now, so at 50, we'd still be like brothers. I think we could do it,' he said. 'I think it would be cool to be up there at 50 years old, still doing the same stuff, still singing.' He laughed. 'Maybe not doing as much choreography, we'd have brittle bones to contend with!'

The 'brotherhood' of Backstreet Boys is something the group's members take very seriously. They refer to it all the time. Like any relationship, it's something they work on constantly and never take for granted. Back in the days when they were all a little younger, much less experienced, and still squashed on a bus together taking them to their next performance, arguments would inevitably erupt. AJ explained that Backstreet Boys have a creed never to walk away angry and never to let a problem fester until show time. No matter what, he's said on several occasions, difficulties are always resolved with a hug before the start of a show.

The strength of the relationships they've built up among themselves is Backstreet Boys' chief asset in their quest for longevity. 'I think, number one, in order to stay together for a long time you have to have communication,' said Nick. 'You have to actually be able to talk with each other. I think we established that pretty much a long time ago. We make sure that we always talk things out.'

Jealousy, Backstreet Boys say, is not an issue among them. Even Nick's popularity among the world's teen magazines does not cause any resentment among the other four members of the group. 'If Nick gets the front page of anything that's just great publicity for the Backstreet Boys,' explained Kevin. 'That's how we look at it.'

Adds Nick, 'We treat this basically like a family of five brothers. We just make sure that anything that pops up we nail it right in the butt. That's why we really never have problems.

'That's why we're so determined and we feel so strong that we're going to stay together for a long time.'

in North and South America, they're already beginning to notice that their music is reaching out to all different sorts of people. 'I'm seeing a lot more guys than we ever really had at our shows on previous tours. Guys can relate to our music in some ways such as using it to, maybe, go on your first date. Guys can speak through our music as we probably did when all of us were younger,' says AJ. 'Music is the universal language. If you can't speak something, maybe you could play a tape or play a song. For guys, I think it's easier to have a girl listen to a song than for me to verbally say how I feel towards her. Plus we have fathers, grandfathers, young boys, and guys of all ages coming to our shows. Our show is for everybody and our music is for everybody. Guys, girls, young, old – it doesn't really matter.'

'I hate the way we're classified as one thing,' commented Nick. 'I think with the Backstreet Boys our music is for everyone.

Another pitfall for many young stars is the temptation to act up in public and risk attracting the attention of the world's tabloids. Backstreet Boys have never claimed to be angels, but they're always aware of their responsibilities to the group and to the fans who buy their CDs. 'There's definitely been a lot of temptations, but I think the fact that we all come from very wholesome families, [we] pretty much know how to separate the good from the bad,' said Nick. 'We've always had our heads on straight.'

'We look out for each other,' adds AJ 'We've got our friends and our family to keep us grounded and, like Nick said, keep our heads on straight. We're not perfect. We don't profess to be perfect. We just try to live our lives in a way that will make our families proud and not embarrass us and not make mistakes. Again, we're not perfect. So we just try to do the best that we can.'

'There are very few times when we're not on stage,' Kevin observed. 'When people know who you are, you're basically on stage whether you're walking down the street or you're doing an interview.'

The group has always said that their music is for everyone, so one of their goals is to continue to reach new people with their songs. By growing along with their fans and moving into new markets

'As long as it makes you happy, that's all that matters.'

US & UK Discography

Singles

'We've Got It Goin' On'
Released US: October 1995/Released UK: October 1995
Highest US chart position: 69/Highest UK chart position: 54

'I'll Never Break Your Heart'
Released US: June 1998/Released UK: December 1995
Currently on release in US/Highest UK chart position: 42

'Get Down (You're The One For Me)'
Not yet released in US/Released UK: May 1996
Highest UK chart position: 14

'We've Got It Goin' On'
Re-released UK: August 1996
Highest UK chart position: 3

'I'll Never Break Your Heart'
Re-released UK: November 1996
Highest UK chart position: 8

'Quit Playin' Games (With My Heart)'
Released US: June 1997/Released UK: January 1997
Highest US chart position: 2/Highest UK chart position: 2

'Anywhere For You'
Not yet released in US/ Released UK: March 1997
Highest UK chart position: 4

'Everybody (Backstreet's Back)'
Released US: April 1998/Released UK: August 1997
Highest US chart position: 4/Highest UK chart position: 3

'As Long As You Love Me'
Released US: November 1997/Released UK: September 1997
Highest US chart position: 4/Highest UK chart position: 3

Albums

Backstreet Boys
Released UK: September 1996
Highest UK chart position: 12
We've Got It Goin' On/Anywhere For You/Get Down (You're The One For Me)/I'll Never Break Your Heart/Quit Playin' Games (With My Heart)/Boys Will Be Boys/Just To Be Close To You/I Wanna Be With You/Every Time I Close My Eyes/Darlin'/Let's Have A Party/Roll With It/Nobody But You

Backstreet Boys
Released US: August 1997
Highest US Chart Position: 7
We've Got It Goin' On/Quit Playin' Games (With My Heart)/As Long As You Love Me/All I Have To Give/Anywhere For You/Hey Mr DJ (Keep Playin' This Song)/I'll Never Break Your Heart/Darlin'/Get Down (You're The One For Me)/Set Adrift On Memory Bliss/If You Want It To Be Good Girl (Get Yourself A Bad Boy)

Backstreet's Back

Released UK: August 1997

Highest UK chart position: 2

Everybody (Backstreet's Back)/As Long As You Love Me/All I Have To Give/That's The Way I Like It/10,000 Promises/Like A Child/Hey Mr. DJ (Keep Playin' This Song)/Set Adrift On Memory Bliss/That's What She Said/If You Want It To Be Good Girl (Get Yourself A Bad Boy)/If I Don't Have You

Video

Live In Concert

Released US: July 1998/Released UK 1997

Let's Have A Party/End Of The Road/Just To Be Close To You/I'll Never Break Your

Heart/Ain't Nobody (Instrumental)/I Wanna Be With You/Anywhere For You/Darlin'/10,000 Promises/Boys Will Be Boys/Get Down (You're The One For Me)

Backstreet Boys: All Access

Released US: June 1998

Everybody (Backstreet's Back)/As Long As You Love Me/All I Have To Give/Quit Playin' Games (With My Heart)/Get Down (You're The One For Me)/Anywhere For You/I'll Never Break Your Heart/We've Got It Goin' On

CD-ROM

Everybody (Backstreet's Back)

Released in US and Canada: June 1998

Acknowledgments

My heartfelt thanks go out to Howie, AJ, Kevin, Brian and Nick who remain as kind, patient and generous today as they were in the beginning. Success couldn't have happened to a nicer bunch of guys. I'd also like to say thank you to the crew at Wright Stuff Management, Transcontinental and Jive Records for all their help. Many thanks to Tamara F., Harriet P. and the folks at Virgin Publishing for putting their faith in me. I also owe an enormous debt to the bad boys of Fairfield for the loan of a laptop computer in my darkest days. Finally, the completion of this project would not have been possible without the support of my own true love, Peter, who kept me fed, clothed and reasonably sane throughout its duration.

Picture Credits

All Action
Todd Kaplan: 1

Alpha
Mark Allan: 44, 56, 58, 59, 63, 93
Hollywood Scene: 6, 88, 94

Corbis
Marko Shark: 3, 14, 15, 30, 33 (top), 36, 52, 90, 96

Famous
Hubert Boesl: 25, 71
Casper: 20, 82, 85
Des Clarke: 60
Fred Duval: 16, 19 (top), 49 (middle), 53, 70
Arjan Kleton: 21
Ralph Ottis: 22
Ian Yates: 50

LFI
David Fisher: 7 (top left), 23
Ilpo Musto: 84

South Beach Photo Agency
P. ZonZon: 7 (middle), 10, 19 (bottom), 27, 32, 33 (bottom), 49 (bottom), 69 (middle, bottom), 73, 74, 75, 76

Pictorial Press
M. Gert: 9, 37, 39, 40, 49 (top), 69 (top), 83 (top)
Jeffrey Mayer: 42-3
Rott: 57

Redferns
Paul Bergen: 4
Grant Davis: 89
Michael Linssen: 77
Simon Ritter: 54, 55, 62
Sue Schneider: 38

Retna
Roslyn Gaunt: 5, 7 (bottom right), 19 (middle), 33 (middle), 51, 67, 72, 81, 91
Steve Granitz: 7 (bottom left), 8, 64, 65
B. Khan: 7 (top right), 34, 47, 80
Janet Macoska: 11, 18, 45, 66, 87, 92
C. Vooren/Sunshine: 24, 26
Theodore Wood: 29

Rex Features
Pat Pope: 17, 78, 83 (bottom)
Brian Rasic: 46
Rex Features: 13, 31, 35, 41, 68, 86